MORE THAN JUST CELLULAR

& Other Musings on Life Past, Present, and Eternal

CHUCK HOLMES

Published by: CS/Books, a part of Corporate Strategies, Inc.,
Atlanta, GA

Library of Congress Cataloging-in-Publications data is available
on request.

ISBN-10: 0 578 49079 3

ISBN-13: 978 0 578 49079 3

First Edition, 2019

Introduction

You can blame this on my grandchildren. At least the younger ones.

Several years ago, it occurred to me that, unlike the first two grandchildren, the younger two were not going to have equal access to their grandfather's wisdom. While they might have considered that a good thing, I didn't. So, I began to write blogs, striving to create a trove of grandfatherly thought that they might access at a later time, if and when they should feel the need of it.

The result, so far, has been about 100 blogs dealing with a range of subjects, from societal changes to politics to memories of what used to be. Some of them are just whimsical. However, they all have this in common: they are all informed by the roles I've had in my fairly long life. I've been a son, father, husband, grandfather, employee, employer, Sunday School teacher, political consultant, lover, lovee, and giver and receiver of gifts. They are all, always to some degree and often to a great degree, personal.

Because they are personal, the reader might learn more about me that he or she really wants to know. I'm old, white, male, Protestant, Liberal, introverted, and sometimes without patience. However, my hope is that, although my characteristics infect each of these essays, there is a greater scope. The few that I thought were pure self-indulgence, I cut out.

Others that were dropped included almost all of those that were politically motivated. During the years I was writing these—2016-2018—our country was going through what I considered a political disaster. A candidate, running on a platform of "I hate the people you hate!" won the presidency. The political divide and the economic divide both widened. And I felt moved to write about what I saw happening. But very few of those essays appear here, for a couple of reasons.

The first is that some of them, like the Abrams-Kemp campaigns in Georgia, are acutely topical. In my opinion, Kemp ran a divisive, essentially fact-free campaign. And he won. For those of us in Georgia, it's going to be a long four years. For the people in the rest of the nation, it's not a matter of great concern. If the piece didn't seem to have some sort of broader application, I cut it out.

Similarly, if the pieces about Trump didn't have a truth (in my opinion) beyond "I don't like Trump." I cut it out. It is my fond hope that years from now someone, perhaps one of my grandchildren, might pick up this book and not wonder about the omission. The administration of Donald J. Trump will be, to that grandchild, a vague and distant memory, and the damage that it did will long before have been repaired. There's no reason I should remind anyone of this political time.

The Internet gives everyone a platform. However, it doesn't necessarily provide an audience. I'm indebted to those who read these when they were originally thrown into the cybersphere and encouraged me. I'm equally indebted to those who are taking the time to read them now. I hope they somehow make your day brighter.

More Than Just Cellular

I was thinking about nude beaches.

That, in itself, is strange since I have never been to a nude beach, don't know anyone who has, and would probably be very uncomfortable if I did. What I was thinking is that if you went to a nude beach you would probably embed mental images in your brain that you would have great difficulty erasing.

That's because most people look a lot better with their clothes on.

But the more I thought about it, the more I realized that there was a deeper, perhaps even profound point to be made. It's that beauty is not really skin deep, and that's probably a really good thing.

For instance, if I were to go to a nude beach, I would see groups of cells more or less artfully arranged (some more, some less), wrapped in some different kinds of cells infused with more or less pigment. I would be seeing them at a single moment in time, the victim of whatever gravity and bad habits might have done for them. Some may be beautiful now, but not later. Some may have been beautiful years ago, but not now. However, I wouldn't bet on even the best-arranged group of cells looking that good sixty years from now.

However, when you live with someone a long time, love them a long time it seems that things become much more than cellular.

Today is Linda's birthday. She and I both seem to be having these on a regular basis, and we've both had a lot of them since we got married. There have been even more since I first kissed her on a five-minute-date at Jean Freeman's party. I was the first boy she kissed, and she says that if I play my cards right, I'll probably be the last.

The point, however, is not that we're getting older. We are, and there's not a lot we can do about it. The point is that as we've aged and changed, Linda hasn't become less beautiful than she was all those birthdays ago.

And it isn't that the changes were not noticeable. Some years back her hair decided it was going to be gray, and a few years after that, Linda decided that chemical coloring just wasn't worth it. Now her face is framed by silver-gray hair, but, as the cashiers in the stores keep telling her, it's pretty silver-gray hair. I think so, too.

Nor does she move as quickly as she used to. But that's probably a good thing since I don't either.

The bottom line is, that if we went to a nude beach together, I don't know how she'd look to other people, but she'd still be beautiful to me. Simply because there's something about living and loving together for a long time that makes things go way beyond cellular. Beauty is not reflected from the outside but from the inside.

One Fine Sunday Afternoon

I was watching my grandson's first Tee-ball practice. The coach, a young man, obviously the father of one of the little balls of energy bounding about him, tried to rein them in.

"Everybody run to first base," he yelled, and his team took off. Two things were immediately obvious. The first was that their knees didn't bend when they ran, and the second was that they had no idea where first base was.

He walked over to first base.

"This is first base," he said. And the boys all ran to gather around him. They'd just learned their first baseball lesson: how to find first base.

The rest of the practice went much the same way. They took a group tour of the infield, identifying each of the bases, then home plate and the pitcher's mound. By the end of the hour, they had increased their baseball knowledge immeasurably.

It wasn't until that night, as I was thinking about the practice, that I realized that I could not remember a time when I hadn't known where first base was. Or, for that matter, what a suicide squeeze, a drag bunt or a sacrifice fly was. I have, so far as I remember, always had a working definition of the infield fly rule. But I grew up on a ball field, and—in season—I watched ball games every Wednesday and Sunday afternoon and played baseball every other day.

It wasn't that I was a good baseball player. I chopped my swing, regularly delivering easy-to-catch ground balls to the infield, and my nickname—NoPeg—pretty well described my throwing abilities. I was pretty good with a glove, and that kept me from being totally disgraced on the field. That—and the fact that I came from a baseball family.

In the late 1940s and early 50s, before there was a TV in every living room and when big league baseball was confined to sixteen teams north of Washington, DC and east of Chicago, every town had its own baseball team. Some were professional (at least at some level), like the Raleigh Caps and Durham Bulls, who played in the Carolina League, and the Dunn-Erwin Twins from the Tobacco State league.

That, except for the occasional pre-season exhibition game, was our idea of professional baseball.

But the teams that we followed most closely were our town teams. They were technically semi-professional in that everybody still had a day job, but more than that they were men who had loved baseball all of their lives and refused to give it up.

Our team was the Benson Bulls. We had Jim Thornton catching; he later gave up the position to become a local TV star and in the process launched the career of Jimmy Capps, who spent nearly forty years in the house band at the Grand Ol' Opry. At first was Will Woodall, the owner of a local clothing store, who was built a lot like Ted Williams. But what made the team more important to me was that, on most days, we had Ray Holmes in right field, Howard Holmes in center, and Bobby Holmes in left. At either shortstop or third base, there was Ed Holmes. He was my father.

Daddy was built like an in-fielder, compact and very quick. He was 5' 8" and about 150 pounds almost all of his life, and he could move to his right or his left as quick as a snake. He also had a tendency to crowd the plate, resulting in a concussion and three broken ribs.

So on any summer Sunday, the Bulls took the field against Coats or Angier or whoever they were playing, and they were no longer the manager of the tractor dealership, the owner of the grocery store, or the appliance serviceman at the furniture store. They were baseball players. And strained through sixty years of memory, they were great baseball players.

Most of the games have grown fuzzy and overlapped each other now, but one stands out, apart from the all the rest, because there were two things burned into my memory.

The first was that the starting pitcher – and in those days, that was the same as the finishing pitcher – showed up drunk. I don't know his name, but his nickname was Red Wing, a composite, I suppose, of the color of his hair and his position as a pitcher. He was a left-hander and was a ringer. He was imported from Erwin, and I would imagine somebody was paying him. But on that day he didn't show up ready to work. He staggered up to the bleachers and evidently decided that was as far as he could go. He laid down and spent the entire game flat of his back singing softly to himself. I'm not sure how he got back home.

But the second thing meant more to me. It hadn't been a particularly good game for Daddy. Having gotten on first, he took off at the crack of the bat. But he lost the ball and—thinking it was still somewhere in the outfield—wheeled around second. The shortstop was waiting for him with the ball in his hand. Out three.

But the Bulls, without their starting pitcher and with what Daddy kept calling a "dumb, dumb, dumb play," managed to stay in the game, and – again, as I remember it – held a slim lead going into the ninth. The other team loaded the bases, and it looked like the lead would evaporate. One out. Three men on base. A tired pitcher who wasn't supposed to be pitching. A late Sunday afternoon.

There was, as always, a lot of chatter from the infield, telling the pitcher that he could do it, that the batter couldn't hit, and that nothing would get by the infielders. It was more habit than a testimony of belief.

The pitcher served one up right across the plate and, the batter connected, slashing a line drive—a frozen rope—straight down the third base line, rising from the moment it left the bat. All of the runners took off, confident that the ball would make it at least to the fence.

But Daddy moved quickly to his right and jumped higher than I'd ever seen him, grabbing the ball in the webbing of his glove. He came back down on the bag, leaving the runner standing between third and home with his jaw dropped and nowhere to go. It was an unassisted double play, and it ended the game. The play more than erased his running error; it was the play that made the difference. Daddy was the hero.

It was hard to be a hero back then. Money was tight, never really enough. You worked hard sixty or seventy hours a week, and at the end of the month, there was a good chance that you were no better off than at the beginning of the month, and at the end of the year no better off than the beginning of the year. I don't think Daddy ever lived up to his own expectations.

But on one fine Sunday afternoon, Daddy had made an obvious difference, one that even he could appreciate. I don't remember him ever mentioning it again, but I like to think that as long as he lived he remembered the feeling of that moment.

&

A Long Way from Benson

In the mid-1950s, in the empty room over Creech's Barbershop that served as the remote studio for WCKB, a group of pickers gathered around the microphone and sang the tune that opened every show. It started out:

Howdy, all you friends and neighbors
Out there in radio land.
Momma's doing the washing.
Daddy's hanging 'round like a man.

Then, after cataloging what everybody else in the family was doing, it ended with:

So sit yourself down
And lean a way back,
And listen to the Smile Awhile Boys — James and Hayden.

James was James Thornton, owner of a local grocery store. Hayden was Hayden Ivy, driver of the Benson trash truck. Together, they were the Smile Awhile Boys.

Not named, but arguably the greatest talent in the room and certainly the most durable one was a teenager with an often goofy smile named Jimmy Capps. He played guitar, and in terms of being a musician, he started where most of musicians worked to get to — and most musicians probably don't get there.

The Smile Awhile Boys moved to television with WTVD in Durham, Hayden's name was dropped from the marquee, and James Thornton became Jim Thornton. The show was Saturday

Night Country Style, and Jim Thornton hosted it wearing a pair of overalls.

Jimmy was the featured guitar player.

When he was sixteen, Jimmy dropped out of school, the combination of playing on school nights and the soporific drone of our social studies teacher's voice making it too tough to stay awake. There was some tut-tutting by some parents, including mine, about Jimmy dropping out of school. They didn't realize that he could already do what we were going to school to learn to do: make a living.

Jimmy left Saturday Night Country Style, passed through South Carolina, played with the Louvin Brothers for a while, and then joined the Grand Ol' Opry in 1967. In about a half-century there, he's played with everybody who's anybody in country music. He also became one of the most popular session players in Nashville.

I had the privilege of playing with Jimmy twice. Once when I went with him to the empty room above Creech's Barber Shop. He handed me a pair of maracas and told me to shake them.

The second time was more memorable.

One of the bands I had in high school was called the Hi-Five, simply because there were five of us. We tried to pass ourselves off as a Dixieland band. We did "loud" really well; intonation and other musical niceties, not so much. The Hi-Five was engaged to play a civic club banquet in Erwin, and for a reason I still don't understand, Jimmy agreed to play with us.

After all, he was a professional musician. The nicest thing you could say about the rest of us was that we weren't.

A lot of the crowd recognized Jimmy when we walked in the door; they saw him on TV on Saturday night. I'm sure that raised the expectations. However, the gig went reasonably well for the first half-hour or so. Then it came — literally — to a crashing halt.

Glenn Baily stood up to take his solo. Somehow, his foot hooked under his chair, causing it to fall backward. It hit the stand for Roy Jones' crash cymbal just as Roy was about to hit the cymbal. Roy missed and fell off his throne. Jimmy, who had been leaning back, strumming along, saw Roy fall and started laughing. He laughed so hard, he fell over backward. At that point, with a third of the band on the floor and the other two-thirds laughing so hard we couldn't blow, the show shuddered to a stop. I'm sure that after everybody picked themselves up and stopped laughing we finished the gig, but I don't remember any of that.

There is something else about that night that after sixty years strikes me as significant. Glenn Baily, clearly the best musician in the original Hi-Five, grew up to be a college administrator in a small denominational school in Georgia. Roy Jones, the drummer, ended up owning several automobile dealerships in Eastern North Carolina. Max Johnson became an engineer for North American Telecom. Keith Neighbors, the other trumpet player, taught math for years. I became a writer.

Of the six teenagers making a joyful, if not necessarily tuneful, noise that night in Erwin, one of us was doing what he was really supposed to do. And Jimmy's been doing it ever since.

On March 16 of this year, the Tennessee legislature passed a resolution honoring Jimmy. In reading the resolution they said a lot of nice things about him and called him a legend. It's not the first time he's been honored. He's a member of the Musicians Hall of Fame and the North Carolina Music Hall of Fame, among other things. And, since he's still playing, it's certainly not the last time.

For honors present, past and future, Jimmy, congratulations.

§

My Brush with Homogeneity

If at the age of 10 I had known the definition of homogene-ity I would have marveled at what a pure model Benson, North Carolina was of it. Most of the families who lived in and around Benson had roots that went back well over a hundred years, and except for the fact that some of us were white and others were black, we were all cut pretty much from the same cloth.

It was a town where everybody knew everybody, and I was related to a substantial minority by blood. There were people in my family who could trace the bloodlines for generations and identify my third or fourth cousins. Most of us ate the same kinds of things, talked the same way, and generally didn't understand a lot about the world beyond the South.

In fact, until the Abdallas moved to Benson, we didn't have any family whose last name ended in a vowel.

We were mostly Protestant, although there were a few Catho-lics in town, fewer than twenty, as I remember, and they were all from families that had come to Benson from Lebanon. And we had one Jew, Jake Greenthal.

In all, it was probably the best place in the world to learn about diversity. Simply because it's hard to subscribe to a stereotype when there's not enough of those in any way different from you to make up a ghetto, a group or a mob. For instance, anti-Semitism is essentially impossible when the only Jewish person you know is a small man with jug ears who has a reputation for being kind to everybody. Daddy worked on Saturdays for Mr. Greenthal, and he never had anything but good to say about him.

The same thing was true with the Catholics, although sometimes the revival people would try to whip up some righteous indignation with an anti-Papist sermon. But the Catholics I knew — Libby Massad, and later Shea and Jeanette Badour — didn't seem any more different to me than the Methodists or Freewill Baptists. (In fact, when Shea and Jeanette's father passed away, most of the high school went to the little Catholic Church for the funeral, and as far as I know, nobody suffered any lasting ill effects.)

It was a little more difficult with the black population, not only because there were a lot more of them, but because my grandparents had been raised by people who had grown up during the Reconstruction. One of my grandmothers never grew out of it. One of my grandfathers tried his best to be prejudiced, but—because he cared about individuals—he couldn't quite pull it off. He got really ticked when I had a black singer with one of my bands. The fact that he sounded just like Nat King Cole didn't matter. But not much later, he closed his filling station for several days while he tried to get assistance for a black family who needed food and clothes.

In any event, I had my parents for guidance, and neither of them had much to say about groups. In fact, one of my mother's most memorable sayings was, "You don't look down on anybody, and you don't let anybody look down on you." Words to live by.

Looking back on it, it took a lot of denial to follow the received wisdom regarding race. For instance, that wisdom said that blacks were lazy, but when the large black woman picking cotton in the row beside me picked more than 200 pounds a day (to my 60 or 70), it was hard to say that she was lazy. (Picking cotton was certainly not my calling, but that's another story.) There was also the idea that blacks were dirty; however, they did the cooking in the better homes, and I was partially raised (two days a week) by Leola, whom I not only respected, but loved.

The long and short of it is that it's difficult to subscribe to stereotypes when you see individuals who don't fit the patterns. And, in Benson, what we mostly dealt with were individuals. There was not a flood or a tidal wave of immigration, as some people describe it now. In Benson, it wasn't even a steady drip.

(After I was grown, I found myself on the receiving end of this same kind of prejudice. Some people in the North, again dealing in stereotypes, believed that anyone who spoke with a southern drawl was, at best, a little slow and, at worst, really dumb. I enjoyed the advantage of those low expectations when I was pitching accounts in New York. However, I also discovered my own perceptions of New Yorkers as being brash and rude didn't hold up when I got to know people like the Santoras in Queens.)

I still have some unanswered questions. One of them was why the Abdallas, the Josephs, and the Massads or Mr. Greenthal came to Benson. It couldn't have been anybody's dream of a city with streets of gold. It was rumored that Mr. Greenthal came from Baltimore, and I wonder if his family exiled him to Benson, but I never knew. I did know that all of these people came to Benson and made a contribution. The Abdallas, the Josephs, and Mr. Greenthal all owned clothing stores. The Massads, as I recall, owned several stores over the years, including the wine shop on the corner until Johnston County went dry and all of the alcohol was supplied by bootleggers.

Now I live in a county where you can hear a half-dozen different languages in the checkout line at Kroger. Where there are signs in Korean, Chinese, Arabic, Spanish, and some other scripts that I don't recognize. And I've learned to enjoy it, because these are individuals, just like the people I grew up with, even though they're not from around here. And now, when I walk into Starbucks and see a Muslim lady working on her laptop in a full burqa, I don't feel threatened or catalog all of the things I've heard about the Muslims. The only thing that crossed my mind was, "How do you drink coffee wearing something like that?" Obviously, the lady had the answer to the question, but my Southern reserve has kept me from asking. So far.

Midday Delights

I was raised in a world without pizza. Or pho or tacos or sushi.

However, it wasn't until I was grown and became acquainted with all of the above that I realize that I had come from as rich a culinary tradition as could be found anywhere. I was raised on Southern cooking. And, if the American Nutrition Association is to be believed, I probably shouldn't have lived beyond about age 15. Our five major food groups were salt, grease, sugar, caffeine, and cornbread.

And we didn't do lunch.

When I was growing up, the three meals of the day were breakfast, dinner, and supper, and often supper was what was left over from dinner. I was introduced to the concept of lunch by Mrs. Bailey when I was in the fourth grade. She explained to us that dinner was the largest meal of the day and could be taken at noon or in the evening. I think most of us filed that information under "things we didn't have to worry about."

Measured by today's standard, there were two things wrong with Southern cooking: it had too much of the things we thought made it so good, and we ate too much of it.

Still, strangely, a lot of people lived into adulthood and some even lived to old age. In fact, one of my grandmothers was told that if she didn't quit eating all that pork she was going to have a stroke. She did. At age 75. She still had black hair and all of her teeth, and until the stoke, she could still outwork any of her five daughters. And probably any of her five sons.

Under the heading of "everything old is new again," a number of the trendier restaurants around here are promoting "local sourcing." That was pretty much all we knew. Granddaddy killed two hogs every year, and the hams and shoulders hung so thick in the smokehouse that you couldn't walk between them. Beside the smokehouse was a chicken yard with a single, very cranky rooster and a bunch of hens. Almost everybody had a garden for fresh vegetables in season and canned ones in the winter. No matter how scarce other things might be, we were never short of food.

The root of most Southern flavor was the pig. Things were cooked with lard, seasoned with pork, accompanied by country ham (salt and pork), corned ham (salt and pork), pork chops (just pork) or roast pork (also just pork). Barbeque was a special case; it wasn't something the Southern housewife did, but it was more pork. A typical dinner might be pork chops, very thin and crisp, peas and butterbeans, corn, sliced tomatoes, baked cornbread (also very thin and crisp), iced tea (very strong and very sweet), and some sort of dessert. Because the vegetables were seasoned with pork, about the only thing that today's nutrition Nazis would bless here would be the sliced tomatoes.

(Some foodstuffs made from pig such as souse meat, chitterlings or chit'lin's, and liver stew aren't mentioned above because I've always done my best to forget them.)

Then there was chicken, usually fried. After I was grown and left Benson I encountered the term "Southern fried chicken." We didn't call it that, probably because we weren't aware of any other kind. This Southern fried chicken was in a hole-in-the-wall restaurant in downtown Atlanta, but the memory of my family's fried chicken was enough to pull me in. This chicken had breading made of concrete encasing mostly raw and possibly poisonous chicken meat and was probably cooked by a Yankee.

Another mark of Southern cooking was that things were cooked, not generally raw or steamed. Green beans, for instance, were cooked to death and had an oil slick on top, courtesy of the pork used to season them. The concept of al dente was totally foreign to our family. My dad and his brothers would have probably figured that Al was the brother of Blackie Dente (who played for the Red Sox, the Browns, the Senators, the White Sox, and the Indians, all in eight years).

Another nutritional problem—even though we didn't consider it a problem—was the amount of food we packed away.

Which brings me to one of my fondest food memories. When I cropped tobacco, I worked one day a week for Mr. Cleo Lee. Because Mr. Lee was a friend of Daddy's, I was invited to eat in the house with them instead of bringing my lunch, which was a work benefit then much like medical insurance is today. On the days when they barned tobacco, Mrs. Lee would get up very early and cook what we called dinner — the midday meal. It was usually one or two meats, two or three vegetables, biscuits and/ or cornbread, and a cake or a pie. She'd leave the barn at 11:30 to go to the house to get it on the table. When Mr. Lee and I got there at noon, it was ready. Mr. and Mrs. Lee had both passed "robust" some years back and would have been given serious warnings by a doctor today. But in those days they just had good food and were glad of it. Mr. Lee worried, though, about the fact that I was built like a Popsicle stick. I can still hear him after I had finished the first overloaded plate of food:

"Take out, boy. Take out. You're going to be poor."

So, I took out. And enjoyed every bite of it.

There is a nearby restaurant that specializes in Southern cooking. It's cafeteria style, and on most days the lines are out the door and down the block. Almost none of the servers are from the southern United States; they are mostly Hispanic, but I'm betting that the cooks are from around here. The food is pretty much as I remember it from years ago.

But I don't go there for lunch. The doctor says that I have to watch my salt.

In Times of Sadness

In the South, we knew how to grieve. Our grieving isn't as well documented as the Irish wake or the Jewish family sitting Shiva, but it was every bit as ritualized. With the Irish, the identification was whiskey, and with the Jews, it was covering mirrors and tearing garments.

We had food.

When I was growing up I had the feeling that no death was official until the neighbors descended onto the house bearing food. In Benson, it took no time for the word of a death to reach everybody around, and only a little more than that before the women trooped in carrying fried chicken, ham, potato salad, various vegetables, and cakes and pies.

And there were usually one or more green bean casseroles. They were straight out of several cans: Campbell's Cream of Mushroom Soup, canned green beans, and French's fried onions. I've never met anybody who admitted liking green bean casseroles, but they were always there.

The people always brought more food than anybody could eat that day and for several days after that. Then some people would come back with a second load. Almost inevitably there would be food left after all the people were gone, and it would have to be thrown out.

But it had served its purpose. It allowed the people who cared about the family's grief to actually do something. Looking back on it I don't believe that eating the food was nearly as important as bringing it. A death in a friend or neighbor's family leaves us with very little that's useful to do and almost nothing to say, but the women could always cook.

Along with the food usually came one or two people who stepped in and took over the logistics. They told people where to put the food, they answered the phone, and they shuffled people away from the immediate family after allowing a reasonable time for conveying their condolences. When my dad died, it was my Aunt Hazel who took over. She and my family were related in a variety of ways. She was mother's cousin, and she married daddy's brother; so she was my first cousin, once removed as well as my aunt.

Her relationship with my family had run hot and cold over the years, but when dad died, she was among the first there and the last to leave, and the fact that she answered the phone when I called made me feel like we were in good hands. She was the second person I spoke to after I got home, Mother being the first.

For several days the food was always there, ready for anybody who came to the house. It was what the women did.

The men had a more difficult time showing their care and concern. Some picked up barbecue and hush puppies. Some got chairs from the funeral home. Some brought bags of ice for the sweet tea. But mostly there wasn't a lot for the men to do. However, they always showed up at the funeral home.

Sometime before I was born they quit laying out the deceased at home. I'm grateful that tradition got consumed by the funeral director business. By the time I had to take my place in the lines filing by the caskets, the departed were always in a room at the funeral home. People stood in the room with the casket or on the porch, talking softly. Occasionally you'd hear laughter.

31

This time, the next to the last time I was in that funeral home, daddy was the one that everybody had come to pay their respects to. Being the oldest son, my job was to help receive the people when they came and acknowledge their condolences. It's hard to do when you haven't had time to tend to your own grieving or your family's, but we did what we were supposed to do.

I remember one encounter during that evening. I had stepped out on the porch for a moment and a man I knew came up to me. He shook my hand, shook his head, and said, "I don't know what I'm going to do when my oven breaks, now." My first reaction was, "I don't know what I'm going to do without a father," but I just nodded. After he had walked away I understood what had just happened. In his own way, his grief was just as real as mine, and he had expressed it in the most personal way he could.

Death is too big for us. It leaves us feeling helpless and powerless; so we invent ways to show the living that we do care, that we'll do what we can to help them keep going. It may be fried chicken, or it may be just showing up at the funeral home and saying something.

As inane as the words may sound when they come out of our mouth at times like that, they say in some way that the person in the casket was important to us and that we're sad, hurt, and sorry that that person's gone.

I've been through several of these times now, and each time I learned to appreciate more what it meant to those who grieve. I'm not sure that the tradition will last much longer, at least in a city like Atlanta, not only because everybody lives such busy lives, but because so many of the people we know aren't from around here, and they don't know from green bean casserole, much less fried chicken. But I hope it doesn't go away before I do.

It's a big help to those who are left.

Mother's Day

Sometime during the 1980s, my mother was named "Humanitar-
ian of the Year" by one of Benson's civic clubs. The picture in
the Benson Review shows her standing there while one of the
club's officers, holding a plaque, reads the citation. She stands
there with a slightly amused smile, the same expression she had
in every picture ever taken of her.

I think that while she was listening to the guy reading the citation she was probably thinking that he was like a lot of preachers
talking about the dead person at a funeral: they're in the ballpark,
but they haven't touched any of the bases.

It's very probable that the description of Mother's humanitar-
ian efforts was a lot more high flown than the efforts themselves.
She was more fundamental than foundational. It was this simple:
see a need and fill it.

Mother was a teacher's aide working with special needs children, and she also drove the school bus that took them to their
school in Selma, about twenty miles away. These were children
from poor families that lived in the country between Benson and
Selma, and there were a lot of things they didn't have, some of
them essential.

Mother would see that one of her students needed something, say a pair of shoes. She would go to a local merchant and
explain why that merchant should donate a pair of shoes. And
the merchant did.

I'm sure that there were store owners in Benson who hated to see Mother come into their store, but the dozen and a half kids who rode on her bus were the better for it. They were children—some of them well into their teens—who needed looking out for.

See a need. Fill it.

Mother drove that bus well after she passed the typical 65-year-old retirement age. She drove it when she had some difficulty getting up into it because of her arthritic hip. And she protected her passengers fiercely.

Somebody asked her one time if she wasn't afraid to drive the special needs students. Some of them were much bigger than she was, and their behavior was sometimes unpredictable. Wasn't she afraid of being attacked and injured?

Obviously, the person asking the question didn't know Mother. This was a woman who had— ith our father—raised three sons and could, right up to the last week of her life, pin any of them to the wall with "the look." I imagine all she had to do when one of her students got out of line was give that student the look, and he or she became very orderly.

I knew the look well. Mother and I grew up together. She was a child bride, and I came along three years later. Daddy went to the navy, and there we were. A mother, just turned twenty-one, and a toddler, and a three-room apartment. Mother didn't have a lot to do but raise me, and she really wanted me to grow up to be a gentleman.

See a need and fill it.

She wore out more than one Emily Post book making sure that I knew how to behave, and her lessons weren't lost on me, although they did have some unintended consequences.

Once, when I was about twelve, I went to Broadway, NC for Preacher Calcolt's camp. Once a year, Preacher Calcolt turned his farm into a Bible camp for the local kids, and for some reason, my parents thought it would be a good idea for me to go, the only camper who didn't know all the other campers. On the first day, Preacher Calcolt called me to the front and introduced me as the son of a member of one of his former congregations. He also said that I was a perfect gentleman and that I even bowed when I was introduced to someone. In a single sentence, the preacher ensured that Bible camp was hell for me all week.

Mother had an abbreviated education, and she decided that needed fixing. She started reading, all sorts of books, and she continued until she could no longer hold a book, learning a wide variety of things. She also passed a love of books and reading to her sons. Two of us graduated with English degrees. The third one majored in Art, probably because it wasn't English.

Looking back, I can see that Mother had decided the kind of person she wanted to be, one that her childhood, background, and education had not necessarily equipped her for. It wasn't a matter of putting on airs, but of having qualities that she considered valuable. It was a very early encounter with managing by objective, and it worked for her. It also worked for us.

She knew what kind of men she wanted her sons to be, and she did everything she could to help us be that. And when, during our childhoods and teenage years we didn't want to be the kind of men she envisioned, she just gave us the look. Or she applied hard objects to our rears. And we were all better people for it.

About two weeks after mother died, the three sons and our families gathered in Benson to deal with her belongings. She hadn't left a will; there wasn't enough there to worry about the legalities. She had simply made a list specifying who got what. It's a sign of her influence that we simply took the list and divided everything according to it. We didn't squabble over anything. We wouldn't have dared.

There are people who, when they die, you miss. Perhaps you miss them terribly. And then there are people who die and leave gaping holes in your life that no one nor time can fill. Mother was one of those. It was months after she died that I quit reaching for the phone to call her. And now, after twenty years, I still think about her nearly every day.

Godspeed, Scooter.

I've been wondering why milestones make us so sad and anxious. After all, getting to the next milestone is something we pray for, plan for, and work on. Successfully reaching one should be an unmitigated joy. But, it's not.

This weekend we're celebrating the graduation of our oldest grandchild from high school. In a couple of weeks, he'll begin college, working on yet another milestone. It seems that life is like that, endings and beginnings, one after another.

He's going out into the world better prepared than I was. His education is much better. I had to quit helping him with his math his sophomore year—and I'm not sure he needed the help then. He's much more suited to the world he's entering, a young man with a technological bent living in a technological world. Smart, aware, and capable of dealing with the hundreds of inputs that today's society thrusts on us. By rights, he's ready.

Yet I celebrate with a strong streak of sadness and some apprehension.

Part of it is something we've been dealing with for years. All those things that we hang onto even as the kids grow out of them. There was a time whenever he saw me, he ran up and jumped into my arms. He doesn't do that anymore; he's too big and his beard would be scratchy. I had to give that up years ago, but I'll always remember it.

And I'll remember the time, at a point in his young life when his tastes had outrun his words, when he stood beside the bed, asking for coffee. Then he wanted to go out on the deck. We took our coffee outside, sitting and sipping and staring into the back yard. He looked up at me, nodded, and said with great solemnity, "Nice day." He was about three. It's a day I won't forget but cannot recreate. It can't happen again.

However, it's deeper and more profound than that. I believe it's because each milestone is a demarcation between past and future. The past, no matter whether it was pleasant or not, is certain. As one of the current cliché's has it, "it is what it is." It requires nothing more of us, no decisions, and no wonderings.

The future, on the other hand, is nothing but uncertainty, and I realize that Scooter is going out into a world far more bewildering than the one I entered nearly sixty years ago. Common standards that I thought were cast in concrete have not only crumbled, but the dust has disappeared. Clear cut paths that we were expected to follow (and did follow) just aren't there anymore. Compared to the world that he's entering, mine had no questions at all.

Which leaves me with little that is useful to offer him as he steps off into his new world. In his eighteen years, he's come to expect some sort of sermonizing from PopPop on important occasions (and on some occasions not so important). He's endured them with more grace than could reasonably be expected of a growing boy. So I've been trying to think of what I should tell him in the last sermon he'll hear from me as—by any definition — a child.

I won't ask him to go and make us proud. That's not really his job, but I will ask him to make himself proud, to set good and challenging objectives and do everything he can to meet them. I'll ask him to develop and adhere to a creed that lives up to a word we've almost forgotten: honorable. I'll ask him to make choices with an eye toward ramifications. Too many people are still suffering the effects of the philosophy that preached "if it feels good, do it."

And I'll give him my definition of success. It's changed a lot over the years. At some points, it had to do with money. At others, it had to do with just getting through the day. But, for some years now, it's been pretty constant. It's to be able, when you're old, to look back on the totality of your life and honestly tell yourself, "You didn't do so bad after all."

Penance Where Penance Is Due

I fear that I have sinned against my heritage.

Recently, as I was leaving a group of people, I said, "You guys have a great day."

"You guys?"

That was wrong on several levels. In the first place, several of the people in the group were not "guys" by Damon Runyon's definition. When I was growing up, "guys" was gender specific and didn't apply to what we erroneously called "the weaker sex."

But that wasn't the real problem. The real problem was that "you guys" isn't something that someone with three hundred years of Southern blood bubbling in his veins should be saying. We have a perfectly good word for the inclusive second-person plural: y'all.

All my life I have had an identifiable Southern accent, and periodically I lived in places where I got kidded for it. As a child, I spent time in Philadelphia where it was obvious that I wasn't from around there. As an adult, I've spoken to groups with audiences from all over the country, some of whom commented on what they sometimes termed my "Southern drawl."

I never bothered to defend the way I talked. It was what it was, and if other people wanted to speak in harsh accents with chopped off words, I didn't mind. However, my lapse has led me to want to do something to defend the language I grew up with. And maybe correct some misunderstandings.

The first one is that no Southerner would use "y'all" in speaking to one person. The correct word for the second person singular (as it has been for the last several hundred years) is "you," unless, of course, you're a Quaker. "Y'all" is an inclusive, plural pronoun meaning "all of you." And it's not pronounced "you all," but "y'all." Just one syllable.

Secondly, there is no Southern drawl. There are a whole bunch of them. It seems that the accent, like barbecue, changes about every fifty miles. Mine comes from Eastern North Carolina, and just to the northeast of us on the coast near the Virginia border, you find the "oot and aboot" variety. And in the mountains of North Carolina, it's very different.

When I went off to school in the mountains, I was assigned a roommate named Creed Jackson who was from deep in the North Carolina mountains, an area later made famous among linguists for speaking nearly pure Elizabethan English. It took me a week before I could understand Creed. Unfortunately, at the end of two weeks he decided he didn't care for Western Carolina, college in general, or me, went home and didn't come back. I had to start all over.

Anybody with a decent ear can hear the difference between North Carolina accents and those from Mississippi or Alabama. It takes a better ear to tell what part of each of those states the accent comes from.

The third thing is that we don't necessarily talk more slowly than folks in the north. In fact, my speech is about 25% faster than a normal person's, no matter whether they're from the north or the south. For most people this wouldn't make a lot of difference; however, it has been the bane of announcers for years. I'd write a 30-second radio spot, read it in 30 seconds, hand it to the announcer, and it'd be nearly 35 seconds long. We'd try to get it into 30 seconds a few times, then give up and start cutting copy. And I would be muttering, "I could read it."

It's not that we talk more slowly. It's that our words have no edges. They glide from one to another, connecting words and sentences. I like to think of it as graceful. I've been told it sounds lazy. I guess one person sees the rose and another sees the thorn.

But these things only touch on the most superficial aspects of the Southern accent. It goes much deeper. There is, for instance, the use of archaic forms. When I was young, it wasn't unusual to hear a farmer say that he was going to "hope his neighbor." At least that's what it sounded like. It wasn't until I was involved in what the professor told me was the absolutely essential course in Pre-Shakespearean drama that I learned that the farmer was actually saying "holp," and that was a perfectly good English word for "help." It was just three hundred years out of date.

Then there were some things that pretty much defied explanation. For instance, you could hear a mother say to a small child: "Do you want a pretty, good?" Translated from the Southern, it means, "Would you like a toy, my dear child?"

It's one of the tragedies of our age that, because of mobility and television, regional differences are disappearing. They haven't yet; I still use PowerPoint when I'm doing a seminar or giving a speech—sort of English subtitles for the Yankees in the audience. And I still read authors who write graceful southern speech without resorting to dialect and making it sound like Huckleberry Finn. But, by the time my city-born and city-bred grandchildren are grown, the Southern accent will probably be gone. Even now my grandson's speech patterns sound more like British English than Southern English.

But by then there will be few left to mourn the passing.

That's the reason I almost choked when I realized I had said, "You guys." In an infinitesimally small way, I had hastened the demise of a wonderful tradition.

I confess. But because I'm Protestant, I really have no one to confess to or to prescribe a proper penance.

So, I guess I'll just go and say a dozen "y'alls" and six "Bless your hearts."

Of Church and State

I have always been a stalwart defender of the separation of church and state. I'd like to say that it's because I come from a 400-year-old religious heritage symbolized by Roger Williams stomping through the snow; it's more likely that it's because I couldn't spell Deuteronomy on my fourth-grade spelling test.

Fourth grade was a memorable year for me. Vivian Baily was my teacher, and when she wasn't being my teacher, she was being my mother's best friend. I'd come home from a tough day in the fourth grade and find my fourth-grade teacher sitting there talking to mother. I blame Mrs. Baily for my first nervous breakdown.

In addition to the usual subjects, we had to memorize all sixty-six books of the Bible and be able to spell them properly. Some of them weren't a problem; Ruth, Job, James, John, Jude and a few others. Some were moderately difficult, such as Corinthians and Ephesians. And some were just a bear, especially Ecclesiastes and Deuteronomy.

It didn't seem strange at the time. Every morning we had a devotional, and then we went around the room, letting each student recite a memorized Bible verse. "Jesus wept" was so popular that Mrs. Baily finally banned it, giving me my first experience with censorship.

Then we'd have a prayer. Throughout all of this, one of our class members would get up and go stand in the hall. If I'd been smarter, I would have considered this my first glimpse of the problem in mixing public school and religion. But I wasn't. It was only later that I realized that mixing church and state is largely about exclusion.

I did misspell Deuteronomy on the spelling test, although I did write all sixty-six of them in order. It was duly reported to my parents, and I expected to hear a lot about it, but help came from an unexpected source. My dad wasn't given to expressing strong opinions on much of anything, but he made an exception in this case.

When the subject came up, he told Mother that Mrs. Baily should leave that to the Sunday School and teach us what fourth graders needed to know to get to the fifth grade.

As I grew older, I found that dad's position was very wise. Anybody who looks at the history of established religion can see that when religion and politics get together, politics doesn't get more spiritual or religious. However, religion gets a lot more political. And when it does, religion doesn't concentrate on what I understand our faith should do but attempts to impose its will on others.

For instance, in the fourth grade, we learned that the Pilgrims came to the New World to find religious liberty. There were persecuted in England because they were not part of the "in" religious crowd. So they got on some very small boats and fled. As soon as they landed, they declared themselves the "in" crowd, made people pay taxes to the church, and generally tried to get everybody to behave Puritans. So Roger Williams stomped off in the snow.

The thing that brought this meditation on is the current firestorm regarding same-sex marriage. I contend that whether you're for it or against it, arguing Bible verses is not pertinent. The Bible doesn't dictate public policy (or shouldn't) any more than the Koran. However, the Constitution does guarantee my freedom of religion, which means that if I am opposed to same-sex marriage, I don't have to go out and marry a guy. Having been married to the same person of the opposite sex for 55 years, I don't really worry about that a lot.

And this latest brouhaha brings out once again the biggest problem with politico-religion (or religio-politics). It's always more about what I can cause someone else to do (or not do) than it is about the way I live my life, doing what Christ commanded. If anybody is still wondering what that is, just check out Matthew 25:32 and following. Not a word about what I made somebody else do or kept them from doing.

&

The Pastor Protection Act

A few weeks ago a Georgia legislator announced that he was going to introduce the "Pastor Protection Act." Specifically, the act was going to protect pastors from having to compromise their religious beliefs and perform same-sex marriages.

The first thought I had was how silly this was. Pastors have been refusing to marry people for a variety of reasons for years and will continue to. Some won't marry people who have been divorced. Some won't marry people of different faiths or races. The pastor who performed my daughter's wedding wouldn't marry a couple unless they completed a series of counseling sessions with him. He figured that there were questions that needed to be answered before two people committed to spending their lives together.

The second thought I had was that he obviously didn't know the same pastors I did, the ones I grew up with and the ones I've known since I was grown. They were an assorted lot.

The first pastor I can remember was Reverend Calcolt. He was a farmer six days a week and a preacher on the seventh. It was rumored that the Reverend spoke harshly to his mules, sometimes using words that preachers probably shouldn't use. I never heard him do that. All I really knew was that he shepherded his small flock until the Presbytery moved him to Broadway. We were sorry to see him go.

He was replaced by Reverend McMahon. Reverend McMahon read his sermons from a book, and it was rumored that Mrs.

McMahon picked them out for him. During the week he was a civil servant, and on Sunday, he was a preacher. About once every two months, it was my family's turn to provide Sunday dinner for Reverend and Mrs. McMahon. My father was amazed at how much fried chicken the Reverend could eat for a man who didn't seem to put a lot of energy into his work.

Then, because most of my friends and all of the girls went there, I jumped ship and went to the Baptist Church. Thurmond Stone was the pastor, and whether it was because of my age or because of his dedication, he became something of a hero to me. He preached a good sermon, was respected by his congregants and seemed to live the life he preached. He baptized my dad and me on the same Sunday. It was Dad's first baptism and my second.

Eventually, Reverend Stone was called to another church and was replaced by Reverend Lanning. Reverend Lanning had had, according to the stories he told frequently in his sermons, a wild youth. He told of weekends full of drinking and carousing, of drinking beer, whiskey, and wine (which led my uncle Ray to observe that, mixing alcohol as the pre-Reverend did, it was no wonder he woke up feeling lousy). Then one night he told his friends to let him out of the car; that he would walk the rest of the way home. They let him out on a corner and took off. Shortly afterward, they wrecked the car, and they were all dead. Reverend Lanning decided that this was a message that he had better things to do with his life than drink and carouse.

One of the better things he did was perform our marriage ceremony, just before he left for another church.

Over the fifty-plus years since then, there have been a number of others. Some were better preachers. Some were better pastors. Some were young. Some were not so young. Some, like Bobby Jenkins who was a revivalist and had no congregation, had been preachers since before they could see over the pulpit. And some, like Reverend Lanning, had been jerked forcefully into the ministry. They were of all different stripes, but the thing I believe that they all had in common was this: they were sincere in their calling and wouldn't be threatened by either public sentiment or public policy.

Somehow, the idea of these men (and one woman) in the tradition of Stephen, Peter, Andrew, and a great crowd of others needing special legislation passed to keep them from violating their consciences was just funny. I suppose the legislator doesn't have as much respect for the clergy and their commitment as I do.

I do have one modest suggestion for him though. There's a group of people in Georgia that do need his help. They are not called to their current condition nor are they respected for it. They're simply in it. I'm talking about the 20% of our state's children who are, as the bureaucrats say, nutritionally insecure. They are hungry. If the legislator can do something to help them, he'll be supporting the clergy as well as the religion that they preach.

Is veracity overrated?

My two grandfathers could not have been more different. My father's father was very quiet; so quiet that he almost wasn't there. He'd come home from the mill every afternoon and eat dinner in the kitchen by himself, still wearing his hat. Although I was thirteen when he died, I don't remember him ever saying anything. I've always thought that his keeping grandmother pregnant nine months out of every 24 for twenty years was his form of creative expression.

My mother's father, on the other hand, was not quiet. He always had a lot to say, and some of it was true. One of his co-workers told me when I was about twelve, "If Pop Upchurch had had all of the jobs he said he'd had, he'd be 107." He wasn't 107.

However, I never thought of him as a liar. In fact, I still don't. I can't remember any of his non-factual statements that were designed to improve his position or decrease anyone else's. They were entertaining stories told in an entertaining way. Admittedly, since I was his oldest grandson, and he tended to dote on me, I may be a little biased.

Granddaddy—generally known as Pop Upchurch—was a storyteller, and I found early on that I enjoyed them more if I didn't worry about whether they were true. Generally, there was some truth lurking in there somewhere; however, he overlayered it with so much invention you'd be hard put to find it. I think that the theory was that you shouldn't let the facts get in the way of a good story.

There were the stories of his service on the Mexican border in the Pancho Villa days. I have a picture of him, young, tall, spiffily uniformed and wearing a sidearm. Somebody had written across the bottom of it "a real soldier boy." However, I learned some years back that he had borrowed the sidearm and never heard a shot fired in anger. However, it provided fodder for some really entertaining stories.

And there were the stories of his being on the road. Granddaddy was a driver. He was a partner in a trucking company with his brother-in-law until he decided the business wasn't going anywhere and quit. Uncle Claude went on to build it into a very successful business. Then granddaddy drove buses for Queen City Trailways, running between Raleigh and Myrtle Beach. He drove for them until he was almost ready to retire; then they fired him. He said it was because they didn't want to pay his retirement. They said it was because of something he said to a female passenger. Both of those things may have been true.

However, his millions of miles on the road gave him a lot to talk about. He even made the newspaper when he flunked the driver's license examination. The reporter wondered how somebody who had driven literally millions of miles could fail the license exam. That was easy: he was a good driver, but a poor reader. It was a written exam.

I'm not sure now what part of my memories of him are the real Grover Cleveland Upchurch and what part are memories of his inventions. I'm pretty sure it doesn't matter. He was a figure that still looms large to me. And he left me with a couple of important life lessons.

One was that, although he had very little education, he had a Whitmanesque ability to comfortably hold contradictory ideas. For instance, as a Southerner born in the 19th century and raised by people who lived through the reconstruction, he was a racist, about on a par with other people of his age and region. He was very upset when I hired a black singer for one of my bands. The fact that the guy sounded just like Nat King Cole didn't really impress him. However, he closed his business and spent days trying to help a black mother with several small children who lived in an apartment behind his gas station. He got them fuel and food and then got the Salvation Army involved. So far as I know he neither asked for nor received any credit for his efforts, except maybe in my memory.

The other thing was that if there's something you want, you just keep on keeping on. Granddaddy, the driver, always said that when he died he wanted to be behind the wheel of a new car. A bout of prostate cancer made that unlikely and caused him to close the gas station. But then he went to work for the Pontiac dealer. They couldn't pay him much because he was on Social Security, but they did furnish him with a demonstrator. One morning, when he was 75 years old, Granddaddy got into his new Pontiac demonstrator, backed out of the driveway, pulled across the street, stopped the car and died. He'd had a massive heart attack. I imagine him with his hands on the wheel, looking out the windshield at the sleek hood of the new car, and smiling.

Would he have been a better man if he had adhered more closely to the truth? I don't think so. His inventions were as much a part of him as his soldierly erect posture or the flat top he wore right up until he died. One of the things he left me was the conviction that you shouldn't let the facts get in the way of a good story. And that's served me well for a long time.

The War on Christianity?

It seems that I'm a combatant in a war and didn't even know it. So much for my fabled powers of observation.

Twice last week I was told that there was a war on Christianity, that my faith was under attack. I thought this was a bit strange since more than 70% of the US population self-identifies as Christian. I asked one of the war correspondents to explain this war to me. I have had no difficulty practicing my faith and, so far as I could tell, neither had he.

"There are people in the media criticizing Christianity," he told me. I asked for a few examples, but he couldn't remember any. I could have given him a few, but none of those were criticizing Christianity as much as they were skewering people who used Christianity. Sinclair Lewis' Elmer Gantry is a case in point.

Lewis may have been the most uneven major writer in American literature, but he brought his A-game to Gantry. Elmer Gantry was a totally hypocritical human being, using his position in the church (or churches, since he moved around a lot) for personal gain. Although Lewis left Gantry with a seed of a conscience, no reader would mistake him for a real follower of Christ.

And as best I can tell, none of the "proofs" I've found as I was looking online for battles in this war really indicated that I was in any real danger of becoming a casualty. For instance, there was the Fox News mouthpiece who cited President Obama as one of the enemy because he left the phrase "in the year of our Lord" out of a proclamation. He failed to mention that the proclamation was to honor "Jewish Heritage Month." I doubt any church steeples fell over because of this.

The same is true with the "Merry Christmas" flap. I really don't care what a clerk in a department store wishes me so long as he or she does it with a smile after efficiently and accurately ringing up my purchase. If I were Jewish, I would be confused if the clerk wished me a Merry Christmas, since I would be busy celebrating Hanukah.

Or the "one nation under God" argument. I have no problem with pledging allegiance to "one nation under God," but I don't make the mistake of thinking that it was done that way when I was in elementary school. The phrase was added to the existing pledge in 1954 by politicians to separate us from the "godless communists."

Then, there's the gay marriage argument. Somehow a lot of people want to frame what is essentially a legal issue as a religious issue. Whether you have a problem with the legal union of people of the same sex or not, if you really believe what it says in the Constitution you shouldn't have a problem with the government recognizing same-sex marriages. As a husband of 55 years, I don't find that two guys (or two ladies) getting married threatens my marriage at all—or the dedication that I have to the vows I made 55 years ago.

Try as I might I couldn't find where my faith was really under attack. I can go to the church of my choice as I wish. Or not go. I can pray as I wish and where I wish. I can keep all sorts of books on my bookshelves without fear of being arrested for it. Nobody has to listen to me pray, and I don't have to listen to anyone else pray if I don't want to. The thing I cannot do is dictate to others what they have to believe. I think that's a good thing.

We were taught in grade school that the Pilgrims came to Plymouth Rock for "religious liberty." What our teachers or the history books didn't tell us was that, while they left England to escape religious persecution, the first thing they did here was reestablish it, with the Pilgrims as persecutors. (Which, in a convoluted way, can be said to have inspired the founding of the Baptist Church in what is now the US.)

The people of the Massachusetts Colony are a case study in what happens when religion gets intertwined with the government: Religion becomes more political.

I guess I upset my friends who are combatants in the war when I couldn't take it seriously. If a television program tries to make fun of Christianity (as opposed to a flagrantly self-serving practice trying to disguise itself as Christianity), I will probably be miffed, and in retaliation, I will not watch the show. So there!

However, rather than bring the church into politics, I suggest that we follow the tactics of Christians who lived at a time when there really was a war on Christianity. People were not only losing their jobs; they were losing their lives for their faith. Tertullian, the third-century theologian, published a strategy for the church. He said Christians should live so that the pagans would look at them and say, "Look how they love one another and how they are ready to die for one another."

Certainly a stronger statement than carping about whether we use the right language in what is probably a pro forma statement anyway.

If there is ever a war on Christianity, I hope that I'm one of the first to the barricades. And if, in this country, there's a war on Judaism, Buddhism, or Islam, I hope I am one of the first to the barricades. I believe that for me to practice my faith in peace, everyone else needs to be free to do the same.

Trivializing Important Matters

First a disclaimer: I am not, nor have I ever been, female, Jewish, Black, gay, lesbian, or transgendered. I am an OWG (Old White Guy); so if anybody disagrees with the opinions that follow on the basis that since I am not a member of (insert offended group here), I don't know what I'm talking about, I'll probably agree. But it seems to me that groups with very real complaints spend a lot of energy, political capital, and goodwill on things that don't really matter a lot.

It is, essentially, expending their resources on things that offend them rather than things that affect them.

This week we had the NAACP telling a Georgia school that they needed to change their team's name. They're the Rebels. If the Internet got the story right, we had a school in Mississippi whose marching band was told that they couldn't take the field because their program included a well-known hymn. And we had a foundation from the Midwest saying that Georgia and Georgia Tech should quit offering prayer and devotions to the players. Those were just the things that made the news.

As a contract writer, I lived through the he/she controversy of the 70s which was pushed to ridiculous limits (He or she needs to make an appointment with his or her gynecologist immediately.). I had to add characters in videos just so we would balance gender, race, and other important attributes. And I had to quit telling women (not girls or gals) that they looked particularly nice today because somehow that gets translated to a hostile work environment.

To be very clear, I have always been in favor of equality—gender, race, sexual preference or whatever. I'm also in favor of providing a boost to a group if they have been deprived of equality and need a hand getting to a level playing field. I do not want my faith to impinge on another person's or theirs on mine. Having said that, I'm also very tired of picky people.

Take the Confederate battle flag, for instance. It makes about as much sense to fly the Confederate battle flag at the state capital as it does to fly the French flag over Louisiana's capital. Once upon a time, Louisiana was controlled by the French, but that's over. So is the Civil War. On the other hand, if someone wants to fly the battle flag at his or her (note the political correctness) house, that's none of my business. I'd probably consider him (or her) a jerk, but that's none of his or her business.

The idea of public monuments to the Confederacy and their heroes is admittedly a grayer area, but I believe that it's a part of history we shouldn't forget, and I also believe the people on the monuments had a dimension other than they supported slavery.

On the edges of this issue, we encounter examples of trivialities that destroy good will. I am all for eradicating references to the Confederacy and the flag from the capital, license tags, state holidays, and anything else that has to do with state government. However, when you propose that we sandblast Stone Mountain to rid it of distasteful references, I'm put in the embarrassing position of having to switch sides.

Similarly, telling the band in Mississippi that they can't take the field because their program included "How Great Thou Art" goes way beyond my understanding of the separation of Church and State. And I think if they had Jewish music or Muslim music or a medley of the three, I would feel the same way.

Then there's the Freedom from Religion Foundation. They are on a crusade to get prayer out of the locker room. However, so long as it's voluntary and without pressure, I don't see why the FFRF should care. So far as I can tell, no players have complained. There is the question regarding Tech paying their chaplain $7500, but—to me—that question is not nearly as interesting as why universities pay their football coaches more than they pay a whole herd of professors.

Finally, there are the fringes of feminism. I've never really identified myself as a feminist. I believe that there are differences between men and women, and—as the French say—Vive la différence! But different doesn't mean better or worse; it just means different, two parts that make up the whole of the human race. I'm all for equal pay for equal work, and I applauded when the two women finished the Ranger training.

When my daughter walked down the aisle somebody asked me about "giving her away." I told him that she was not mine to give away. She was her own person.

However, I still occasionally get into trouble with those who operate on the edge of feminism. For instance, having been taught to open the door for ladies and the steadily shrinking number of those who are senior to me, I always do it. One time I opened the door for a young lady, and she glared at me. "I can do that," she said. So I let her.

(A similar incident was handled with much more grace by another young lady. I opened the door for her, and she gave me a smile. Then she grabbed the next door and held it open for me. "My turn," she said. That's probably the sort of equality we should be aspiring to.)

As already noted, I am not a part of any group that has suffered institutionalized social injustice. What slights I have suffered were on a personal level and didn't make a lot of difference. And I don't want to appear insensitive to those who have to deal with it every day. My only point is that, with all the big problems to solve, I think it's strategically sound not to waste ammunition on those that don't really change your lives.

We live in a time when women object to being called ladies, where almost any sports team not named after an animal or weather event is going to offend someone, and where any kind of ethnic joke can end your career. I think we have more important things to do.

So far as team names go, my high school team was the Blue Phantoms. Nobody really objected to that, probably because ghosts don't have a very effective lobbying group.

Does it gotta be this or that?

In the 1940s Sunny Skylar wrote the lyrics to a catchy tune named *It's Gotta Be This or That*. Benny Goodman, Ella Fitzgerald, Glen Grey and a lot of others recorded it. Essentially, it says that things have to be in one of two states: wet, dry; gross, net; got, get. It's toe-tapping fun.

It also makes almost no sense. For instance, it says, "if it's not sis…it's gotta be your brother." Which, of course, leaves out most of the world.

For a song, that's not a big problem. However, it seems that people are seeing the world in the same way: it's gotta be this or that.

This particular musing was brought on by a friend's lecturing me about the proposed treaty with Iran. I had expressed a mildly positive view regarding diplomatic solutions rather than bombing people. "You're no friend to Israel," he said.

I started to react defensively: I've been pro-Israel since 1948 (a fact that has made absolutely no difference to Israel).

Then I started to debate: if being pro-treaty is being anti-Israel, what are those 340 rabbis doing supporting the treaty.

But I did neither. I just asked him if he had read the treaty. He hadn't. I hadn't. Neither of us was really qualified to have an opinion on it. However, in that echo chamber my friend frequents, talking heads have instructed him to be against the treaty because being against it is pro-Israel. And, like the workers in Metropolis, he and his fellows march out and make that argument.

This guy is no dummy. We've been friends for a long time, and he has been known to have original thoughts. It's just that original, nuanced thinking is becoming less and less fashionable. Too much of the world is gearing up for conversation by taking a daily dose of Fox News or MSNBC, both of which are clearly and openly based on ideology rather than news judgment.

We have become the living embodiment of the old and rather a lame joke: there are two kinds of people in the world; those who think there are two kinds of people and those who don't.

We have always had our extremists, bigots, loudmouths, and ideologues. That's not new. What does seem to be new is that we are allowing them to set not only the tone of the debate but the facts of the debate, repeating what they say endlessly until it becomes the received version.

An example (taken from the right simply because it was in the paper this morning and not because this particular problem with truth is exclusive to the right): A story was making it around the blogosphere a few weeks ago that Iran would be inspecting their own nuclear sites. Then the New York Times picked it up, only to publish a modified version almost immediately. They found out that the thrust of the story (that Iran would be responsible for the inspections) wasn't true. The truth was that Iran and the international agency responsible for the inspections would both be involved. In other words, Iran would have representatives in their nuclear facilities when they were inspected.

For a couple of weeks, I didn't see any more about this. This, in the conservative column on the AJC's editorial page, the writer (a staff member at the Heritage Institute) makes the flat statement that Iran will be responsible for its own nuclear inspections. And this will be repeated until a large number of people accept it as the truth.

61

Perhaps this is a product of the age we live in, an age where the questions are just too big to be understood; so the easy answers are just accepted. An age where everybody has a microphone called the internet and can say whatever they want to, whether it's factual or not.

Or maybe it's that we've just decided to give up on thinking. In a memo prepared in the Nixon administration (possibly written and certainly endorsed by Roger Ailes), the writer said: "Today television news is watched more often than people read newspapers, than people listen to the radio, than people read or gather any other form of communication. The reason: People are lazy. With television you just sit—watch—listen. The thinking is done for you." That, unfortunately, and with the addition of the internet, is where we seem to be.

I guess the fact that I've written advertising copy for much of my life has inoculated me from believing everything (or even much) that I read. I know that even the best-intentioned writers have their own baggage of bias that seeps into what they write, and I suspect that there are few who could be truly called "best intentioned." Too many are ax grinders.

When I was a child, you were either for the Red Sox or the Yankees. You either worshipped Ted Williams or Joe DiMaggio. It had to be this or that.

But that was childish then. It's childish today. There's no requirement that we surrender our right to our own opinions, especially if we've made an effort to buttress them with actual facts. I would really be happy to have a conversation with anyone of any stripe who would do just that.

§

Outraged over Outrage

Last week I read *End of Discussion: How the Left's Outrage Industry Shuts Down Debate, Manipulates Voters, and Makes America Less Free (and Fun)*. (Not just the title, but the whole book.)

And I thought how easy it would be to write the same book substituting the word "Right" for "Left."

The authors, Mary Katharine Ham and Guy Benson, write well. For the most part, they don't take themselves too seriously, and they even make a feint at offering an even-handed treatment. They admit on page 9 that "the Right is hardly blameless," then they proceed for another 274 pages to blame the left.

I really expected nothing more or less from them since they are both employed by Fox News. However, in some cases, it seemed that they almost sprained their typing fingers keeping them pointed at the left.

They decried the name calling, without referencing any of the Right's name slinging. That's one place where I laughed. They also had a long chapter on voter manipulation that included a number of potential voter frauds but didn't mention that George W. Bushs' state of Texas sent Jeb Bushs' state of Florida a list of 2000 felons. Florida matched the list against the voter roles for people with similar names and approximate birth dates; the only exact match required was for race. The 2000 felons became a list of over 50,000 people who, by Florida law, could not vote unless they could prove that it was a case of mistaken identity.

(Johnny Jackson, Jr. probably had an easier time than most proving that he wasn't the felon since the right guy—John Fitzgerald Jackson—was still in jail in Texas.)

But that wasn't the part that made me sad. It was that the book title worked as well blaming the Left as the Right (and vice-versa). That's the point to which we've fallen.

I found that there were some places where I was in full agreement with Ham and Benson. For instance, there's the story of one young lady who took off for Africa with a job and landed in Africa without one. This story has been told in the last two books I've read, the other one written liberal-leaning author. It seems that the young lady tweeted what she thought was a joke and everybody else in the world thought was bad taste.

Twitterdom went into action, following her across the Atlantic like a swarm of killer bees. The result, as noted, was that she lost her job, a punishment that in no way fit the crime. In fact, there was no crime. It was just bad taste. And if bad taste were a crime half the people going to the mall would be in jail.

This sort of thing, lynching by bits and bytes, seems to have become something of a sport.

Ham and Benson highlighted another problem that seems to be growing: sensitivity as a weapon of power. In this case, a DJ at a bar in Chapel Hill played a song that a female patron objected to. I'll admit I don't fully understand this story since I've never heard "Blurred Lines" by Robin Thicke. I looked up the lyrics and found that the intro was: Everybody get up, WOO/Everybody get up, WOO/ Hey,hey,hey/ WOO/Hey,hey,hey/WOO.

So far as I'm concerned, we're back to bad taste again. However, the offending line seems to come in the first verse: I know you want it. (I'm surprised that line's still around. It was considered ignorant when I was in high school.)

The offended young lady said that hearing that song "might be a triggering event for some women." She not only complained to the DJ, but also to the manager. The manager issued a public apology and announced that the DJ had been fired. This for playing what had been a number one tune for twelve weeks and Billboard's Song of the Summer.

(The song's popularity again shows the level to which we've fallen, but that's a subject for another time.)

The point is that one person gets offended, raises a stink, and someone—totally innocent, so far as I can tell—gets hurt. Then the offended person feels victorious and goes to look for something else to be offended about.

I get offended, too. Even outraged. And one of the things I'm offended about is that someone could make a lot of money from lyrics like those referenced above. However, I know that I have no constitutional right not to be offended, that my opinions may differ from others, and that my zone of personal influence probably does not extend more than three feet in any direction.

If I'm offended, I may express it, but I shouldn't expect anybody to do anything about it.

This incident raises a number of questions. Why wasn't it sufficient for the young lady to simply ask the DJ not to play the tune? Why did the manager need a sacrificial employee? And the big one, how did this song remain number one for twelve weeks, especially if it was so offensive?

Perhaps in that last question lies the answer to the problem. If we are offended by something, we shouldn't buy it, shouldn't listen to it, shouldn't watch it, and certainly shouldn't make it more profitable for those who are doing it. We have a personal responsibility to protect ourselves from that which we deem offensive, and if each of us does that, much of it will probably go away.

However, we shouldn't become a mob of cyber vigilantes looking for things to scream about so that we can make someone else's life more difficult. That's neither civilized nor smart.

Ham and Benson, bless their little conservative hearts, point out a lot of problems that affect us. The fact that they're terribly selective in their proofs doesn't make the principles any less true.

Which brings me to my final question: when did we start worrying about Right and Left instead of right and wrong?

Papa

Having been a Baptist for most of my life, I haven't paid a lot of attention to the Popes. About the closest I ever got to a real interest was a prolonged discussion of Papal Infallibility I had with a professor at Spring Hill College when we lived in Mobile. It was a civil discussion, lubricated by several bottles of beer, that really didn't change anybody's opinion. He subscribed. I didn't. After that, I still didn't pay much attention to what the Pope said or did.

That is, until Pope Francis came along. He seems to transcend denominationalism and let us stare into what Christianity is really about. In a news clip I saw last week the Pope left the popemobile and walked over to what appeared to be a severely disabled child. He held the child's face and gently kissed his forehead.

If you do it to the least of these...

There are people popping up on the op-ed pages who don't seem to be as impressed with Pope Francis as I am. One Conservative columnist called him the Pope of the left. George Will, who used to impress me, criticized the Pope's comments on climate change. The only really thoughtful piece on the Pope that I've read from the Right was from a Catholic lawyer who pointed out that Pope Francis has not changed the Church's core beliefs. The Church is still opposed to abortion, to divorce, and to any number of other things that society seems to accept.

However, I believe that Pope Francis has taken giant steps in reordering the Church's priorities—or at least its public focus.

Thou shall love thy neighbor as thyself…

I find it sad that we live in a time when basic Christian values are politicized. His statements about feeding the hungry, about income inequality, and about what we are doing to our planet have drawn fire. It seems that he doesn't embrace capitalism sufficiently for some. They would prefer that he be regal, distant, and uninvolved.

Go, sell everything that you have and give it to the poor…

I wonder if it's possible that Pope Francis, in whatever time he has in the spotlight of the Papacy, can create a lasting change in how we Christians see Christianity. We've had social theology, which was essentially a rebellion of the powerless, and we've had Conservative rigidity, which seems more intent on defining who cannot be Christian than dealing with the pain of those who might be. We've had the feel-good theology that tells us that God loves us, but doesn't really require a lot from us. And we've had those who call themselves Christians, but probably couldn't prove it.

I don't know that any of the above is the majority of any group of Christians—right, left, Protestant, Catholic, liturgical or evangelical—but I do know that these are the images that the world sees. And these are the images that cause others to question our witness.

Until we see someone like Pope Francis. No red shoes. No papal palace. An old, obviously tired man, summoning another smile, another touch for those who need a smile and a touch. A man who chooses to eat with the homeless rather than the mighty. A man who stands with presidents and beggars and seems not to be overly impressed with one or to disdain the other.

The clip that stuck with me most vividly was when the Pope greeted a group of children. They were wearing school uniforms, probably from one of the Catholic schools. He smiled and chatted for a moment. Then he said something to the children and walked away.

The reporter asked one of the children what the Pope had said as he was leaving.

"He said, pray for me."

It made me, Baptist that I am, want to have the spirit of Pope Francis.

More than a Label

Several months ago we had occasion to file a police report, and DeKalb County wanted to send someone out rather than take it over the phone or have me come in. About 10 o'clock that night a police officer showed up at the door.

He came in. He was very courteous and efficient. He took our report and explained how we could get a copy of it. The whole thing took probably twenty minutes.

The next time I encountered him was on the news. Officer Kevin Toatley had been killed in a traffic accident, hit head-on by a driver heading the wrong way on the freeway. Officer Toatley was driving home. That afternoon he had survived a police chase that had ended in a shootout not very far from our house.

According to the news reports, he had called his wife from the scene to tell her he was okay. A few hours later he was killed on the highway.

Hardly a day goes by that we don't hear about someone being killed. A policeman. A teenager. A homeless person. A senior citizen. The fact that our information is filtered through the flat screen of the television set makes it easier to absorb that someone with that particular label is dead without thinking about the fact that this was a person with—until that point—a future, with a family, perhaps with children who expected to see their father or mother come home.

I didn't know Officer Toatley except for those twenty minutes he was in our house. He came because we had been wronged and needed to file an official report. I was impressed by him and by his ability to do his job, as minor as the part of it dealing with us might have been.

And since then I've had difficulty when I hear of another shooting or car crash getting beyond the fact that we seem to depersonalize them by giving them a label. Perhaps it makes it easier to live in a world that's gone far too violent.

Violence is nothing new. Years ago, a man I had gone to school with, one of the mildest and most unassuming people imaginable, walked into his barn and was shot to death by his son. The headline in the newspaper called him by name.

It's not that violence exists, but that it's so prevalent. And I'm afraid we're becoming desensitized to it, to the point that otherwise normal people are on the Internet with posts in praise of somebody who took a shot at a shoplifter.

I believe, based on our very brief encounter, that our community lost something important when Kevin Toatley was killed. He was a man who did his job and went home to his family. He was, I'm sure, looking forward to seeing his children grow up. The headline read, "Officer killed in Crash." But that's very limiting. He was an officer. He was also a husband, a father, and as best I could tell, a very decent human being.

It would probably make us think more and perhaps do more if we quit killing labels and recognize that behind every one of them is a person who's important to those around him or her. They're not labels; they're people.

$$\mathcal{G}$$

Meet Joe.

My introduction to Joe was a little unusual.

It was my first night as a volunteer at Clifton Presbyterian's homeless shelter. My daughter Leslie had been volunteering there and suggested I join them. On that first evening, the people who ran the kitchen quickly and accurately appraised my cooking skills and assigned me to the serving/cleanup crew.

As I was setting a plate of food in front of one of the homeless men, someone grabbed my wrist. The hand holding my wrist belonged to a man with a ragged gray beard, a wrinkled face, a ragged coat, and what I believe was fear in his eyes.

"The food's not poisoned," he said.

I thought I had misunderstood him, but I hadn't. He said it again.

"The food's not poisoned,"

"No, the food's not poisoned," I replied. I didn't know what else to say. He was still holding on to my wrist.

"Pray for me," he said.

"I will."

And that was my first encounter with Joe. I don't remember his last name if I ever knew it. Nor what he had been before his brain detached him from the real world. Joe had fallen through any number of cracks in the system we have for dealing with mentally ill people. He was paranoid and fear seemed to go with him wherever he was.

There were still shreds of what Joe had been. For instance, he could still play the piano, and he accompanied the Christmas Carol sing-alongs at Clifton. There was a rumor that he had been a professor at Tech, but that probably wasn't much more than a rumor. Essentially, Joe was what I saw when I looked to see who was holding my wrist: a man who had to struggle to deal every day in a world that didn't want to have much to do with him.

But Joe, along with some of the others who gathered at Clifton every evening for a meal, a shower, and a place to sleep, taught us some lessons. And perhaps the greatest service that Clifton did, in addition to providing a bit of safety and comfort for men who otherwise had none, was that anyone who volunteered there never thought about the homeless the same way again.

At a distance, it's simpler to deal with the label. We lump them into statistical groups and discuss them as societal problems. But when you serve them dinner and sit and talk with them, you find that homelessness is a condition rather than a description; it affects all sorts of people. There was the computer programmer I talked with who still had neat clothes, who could still carry on an intelligent conversation, and who, because of his disconnects with reality, couldn't hold a job. He'd come to Atlanta when he lost his last job somewhere in the north, hoping to find work. But he found himself homeless.

I don't know how many individuals and institutions had failed Joe in his descent from the child learning to play the piano to the homeless man who slept at Clifton every night and had to leave every morning. Certainly, the governments had failed, seeing him as a problem to be solved rather than a person to be helped. Perhaps his family had, too. Or his friends. There's no way of knowing, but I do know that, except for Clifton and the people who ran it, Joe was alone and adrift.

One day Leslie went into the sandwich shop across the street from her office and saw the girl behind the counter backed up about as far as she could get. Joe, in his ragged clothes and more ragged beard, was begging for a sandwich. He was, to the girl, a scary sight and a crazy man. Leslie recognized him. She bought him a sandwich and took him to a table, where she sat with him while he ate. Then he left to wander until the bus from Clifton picked him up in the evening.

To me, that was the starkest lesson of all—what those two young women saw, and because of what they saw, how they reacted. The girl in the sandwich shop saw a homeless man, unkempt, and possibly dangerous. Leslie saw a troubled man who was grateful for every crumb of compassion offered him. That's the sort of thing that happens when we can see beyond the labels and recognize the humans behind them

Joe died some years back, and his name is memorialized at Joe's Place, some apartments for men who, unlike Joe, are able to overcome whatever has made them homeless and to work themselves back into what we think of a normal life.

Rage is the new black

In this Year of Our Lord 2015 it appears that if you wish to be in step with the times, you have to be ticked off at something or somebody. If you frequent social media, it's obvious that rage is all the rage today.

I have a difficult time enlisting in other people's anger armies; so I usually just ignore the memes with aggressive comments or foul language. However, either I have become more observant or the campaigns are tipping further and further into the stupid bog.

For instance, there was one post being shared on Facebook last week that was attempting to rouse some rabble because, according to whoever wrote it, Social Security checks were going to be referred to as Federal Benefit Payments. I'm not sure what the poster wanted me to do about it—man the barricades, picket the local Social Security office, burn my Social Security check? (I can guarantee that the last thing is not going to happen.)

However, I don't have to leap to any of the above. First, because I really don't care what they call the money they deposit for me each month. As my brother Pat said, "They can call it dog food for all I care."

The other reason is that the poster of the meme either didn't know the facts or didn't care about the facts. The facts are that Federal Benefit Payments are a broad class of payments (including Social Security), and have been called that since the 1930s when the legislation was passed.

Another crisis averted.

Other rabble rousers choose much more sensitive subjects. There was a meme showing somebody desecrating an American flag. My generation was raised to honor the flag, to die for it if necessary. We show our flag on appropriate occasions, and I still go to great lengths not to let it touch the ground. I object to people not treating our flag with respect. So I should enlist in this particular anger army? Nope. The meme isn't posted to promote the proper respect for the flag; its message is that there are people out there we're supposed to be angry at, although the poster doesn't suggest what we're supposed to do with that anger.

The list could, of course, go on. Check out your social media page on any given day, and you'll probably find a dozen or more of these posts, some more idiotic than others, but none particularly useful, all asking you to get mad at something or somebody, as if anger without action were a solution to those things. If that were as far as it goes, I'd just go back to being a noncombatant in the rage wars. But it doesn't seem to stop in the cyber world.

Last week, on one thirty-minute news show, there were two road rage stories. In one story a woman was shot in the back but managed to get her Corvette off the expressway without killing anybody else. She's recovering in the hospital. The shooter has not yet been arrested. In the other, more tragic story, a four-year-old girl was killed.

I believe that what we see on the Internet and what is happening in the real world are connected. There are people whose primary purpose is to generate anger and unrest over all sorts of things, some of them even true. Most of us are armchair anger mongers, and all that this does is contribute to the growth and well-being of our ulcers. However, there are a few who take it to one of the next levels, the most extreme being using one of our freedoms to deny someone else of their freedom or their life.

Since I have a real distaste for people who pose problems without posing solutions, I would suggest the following when you see one of these "look what they've done to you now" postings:

1. If it's not important, not true, or doesn't point to a legal remedy, ignore it. That'll take care of about ninety percent of what you see.
2. If it's important, true, and appears to be something you can do something about without having to serve time if you're caught, take action.
3. If your system really needs something to rage at, here are some suggestions:

    • The fact that so many in the United States, black and white, are raised in an environment of hopelessness.
    • The fact that so many look at these people, tuck their smugness around them, and self-righteously say, "it's all their fault. If they'd just made the right decisions they wouldn't be there."
    • The people who are enriching themselves at all levels of government at the expense of the citizens.
    • The fact that we still talk about American exceptionalism as we fall further behind other countries in health care, in the care of our families and seniors, in education, and in upward mobility.

And that list, too, could go on. However, the important point is that if we're going to rage against something, we should at least look for a solution. Enough of this Henny-penny stuff.

$\mathcal{G}$

In Praise of Old People

I taught Sunday School for about forty years, and for most of that time I was guided by a simple rule: I didn't teach anybody under four feet tall or over fifty years old. The first part of that rule was because I'm not a good match for children; I tend to talk to them as if they were very short adults. The reasoning behind the second part was two-fold: I wasn't sure I had anything to teach people who had lived longer than I had, and I really didn't believe that most of the older Baptists would be comfortable with what I considered a very orthodox, but nonliteral approach to the Bible.

However, when we moved to First Baptist I was, for the first time in years, without a class to teach, and the word must have gotten out. I received a call from Lorenzo Acevedo asking if I wanted to audition to be the teacher for his class. He made it very clear that this was an audition; if they didn't like me, they'd let me know.

Evidently, my trial lesson went reasonably well because the class decided to keep me. I found myself teaching the oldest Sunday School class in the church. The quip was that you went to Holmes' class; then you went to heaven. The quip would have been funnier if it hadn't been so true.

The class and I were together for ten years, and they seemed to be up for whatever I could bring them. One year we did a complete survey of the Bible, and one of the members told me that it was the first time he'd ever read the Bible all the way through. Another year we studied the history of our denomination, something that most life-long Baptists know very little about. I think a lot of what we studied was new information to the class members. Probably a lot of them were uncomfortable with parts of it.

Every Sunday morning was a joyous occasion for me. Not only did I get to go to one of the few places in the world where I still lowered the average age, but I got to study with and teach some of the nicest people I've ever known. They said that they learned something from me.

I know I learned something—probably a lot more—from them. I learned how people successfully grow old.

I don't like being old. I come from a long line of people who—however unsuccessfully— vigorously fought aging right to the end. My father celebrated the 25th anniversary of his 39th birthday. And about the time I started teaching the Old Folks' class, I was staring down the barrel of the future and not liking what I saw at all.

But it's hard for a sixty-year-old person to feel really sorry for himself when he's talking to a ninety-year-old. It's hard to really focus on your own increasing aches and pains when your class comes in—smiling and chatting—on canes and walkers. And it's hard to get your back up when you disagree with someone when each week you have twenty people, each with more life experience than you have, listening intently and looking as if they thought you made sense.

But those are generalities. There were some very specific things I learned from my Sunday School class.

One is that just because you're old, you're not done. These were people who had accomplished things. They had raised families. They had been executives, school teachers, and librarians. They had been a vital part of their community. Now that they were retired or physically unable to do some of these things, they still found something they could do. I imagine they had their own complaints about getting old, but they didn't share them with me. Except for the modern music in the blended service, there was very little they complained about.

They actively loved each other. This may have been a generational function or because of where they had grown up, but they were significantly more involved in each other's lives than a lot of city dwellers. If somebody was missing from the class on Sunday, several people could tell us why because they had called and checked on them.

They were respectful. People could disagree in that class without rancor. For a couple of years, our class had a Catholic member, the product of a mixed marriage: the husband was Catholic and the wife Baptist. Each Sunday they went to Mass, then came to Sunday School. The husband was articulate and well-schooled in the doctrines of his faith, and I made a point of asking him to offer another point of view when we dealt with something that our denominations differed on. The class listened, and if any of it bothered them, they kept it to themselves.

Essentially, they were dealing with old age by being determined to live until they died, not giving a bit of ground they didn't have to.

One of the first people I met on the Sunday of my audition lesson was Bill Williams. And the first thing I noticed about him was that he had to use one of those metal canes with three legs on the bottom. The second thing I noticed was Bill didn't let it touch the ground. I'm guessing his wife and his doctor had impressed on him the importance of carrying a cane, but somehow he'd missed the message about using it.

And Bill also embodied another quality that seemed to be generously distributed throughout the class: humility. He was a man who had accomplished a lot of things in his life. He'd been a colonel in the Army during WWII. He'd stayed married to the same woman since they both were young. He had held executive positions in a number of companies and had prepared well for what turned out to be a long retirement. But you would never learn much about any of that from him.

In his last days, Linda and I would occasionally visit Bill and Nell. The women would talk flowers, and Bill and I would touch on the news of the day. Every time, when we left, Bill said the same thing: It's really nice for folks like you to come to visit a fellow like me.

I said the same thing about him when I gave the eulogy at his funeral.

These were just people, not a saint among them. But when I go out into the world today, especially in Atlanta traffic, or when I'm on the internet, I wish that there were a lot more like them.

I'm trying to grow old like they did.

Holo Graphic, Batman. It's the Dead Guy Talking.

It seems that the big news on the funeral front these days is holographic eulogies—technology that allows a holographic image of the dear departed to get up a say a few words to the folks at the funeral. According to the funeral industry trade papers, this is a way for funeral homes to recoup some of the revenue they're losing because cremation has become the finish of choice for so many people.

As the head of the hologram company says, "If you're a funeral director, and they choose an $800 cremation over a $14,000 funeral, you have to find another way to add value."

I personally think that it's one of the worst ideas I've ever heard. But I don't have to worry about it. The hologram company is marketing its services to "high wealth individuals," which they define as someone with a net worth of more than $30 million. I'm not there yet.

The idea of dead people doing their own eulogies does solve a couple of problems. We've all been to funerals where the preacher doesn't appear to have met the person in the casket before he or she passed. The departed is sent on its final journey on a pallet of platitudes and nobody leaves the funeral feeling any better for what's said.

Or, conversely, where the preacher does know the deceased, but couldn't really tell the truth about him or her without fearing a slander suit. So, back to the platitudes.

However, if we substitute the dead guy doing his own eulogy, we may find the cure far worse than the illness. For instance, I can imagine hearing something like this:

"I guess you're all surprised to see me. It's a miracle of technology. But you're not nearly as surprised to see me as I am to see my old partner, Kenny. Especially after all the things you said about me. And you thought you were talking behind my back.

And, Francis, now that I can finally get in a word edgewise, there are a few things I'd like to tell you…"

Or, we might find that the guest of honor was not a bit more interesting in the deceased version than he was in the live one and that the holographic eulogy was a serious waste of money, money better spent on food for the wake.

I believe there's a better solution, one that solves the problems without creating what could be an infinite stream of unintended consequences. It takes two things.

The first is that you get in really tight with a preacher. Make sure that he knows who you are and thinks well of you. (Alternately, you could choose someone else to do the eulogy, anybody you could depend on to show up and say good things about you.)

The second is the harder one: give them some ammunition. Do some good things in your life that make the eulogy believable.

I'm convinced that everybody gets to choose the way they're remembered. If we want to be remembered as someone who cared for his fellow man, we have to actually do things that demonstrate that we care for our fellow man. What they say about us when we are dead is—unless we want to be sent off with platitudes—dictated by the way we live our life.

Years ago, I started a short story with the following line: *Andy Tatum was 35 years old when he began to worry about his eulogy. He decided he had to start living his life more intentionally.*

I'd just been to my father's funeral. The Baptist Church in my home town had recently called a new pastor, and he didn't really know dad. It wasn't his fault. Just a circumstance. There were a lot of good things that you could say about Dad; he was a good man who could be trusted and depended on. He didn't smoke, drink, or cuss. He was very good at what he did. He valued his family, nuclear and extended. A lot of things. None of which came up at the funeral.

Dad had missed thing number one, which meant that his memorial didn't get the full benefit of thing number two.

I'm sure that there are a lot of people who think that it doesn't matter a lot; if you're dead, you are beyond worrying about what the living say about you. That's probably true, but I still think it's important, sort of the cherry on the top of the sundae. It gives those who care one more way to honor your memory and remember your life.

But I'm convinced that my funeral eulogy is not a DIY job.

Why indeed?

Last week, in one of my morose moods, I remembered the final lines from Edna St. Vincent Millay's Lament: Life must go on; I forget just why.

In college, wallowing in beatnik angst, I would often mutter that line, attempting to look world-worn and profound at age 19. I also spent a lot of hours trying to write a line as bleak as that one. I never succeeded, probably because at age 19 I didn't really know what Edna was talking about.

The poem is in the voice of a woman who is telling her two young children about the death of their father. Most of the poem has to do with linking the father to the children (From his old coats/I'll make you little jackets;/I'll make you little trousers/from his old pants.) Only in the last two lines does her reflection turn inward: Life must go on; I forget just why.

For most of my life I was busy being a husband, father, employee, employer, and getting the next thing done, the next bill paid, or the next child carted to wherever that child needed to be. Purpose wasn't a question in my life.

However, when I got old and the children were grown and working for a living was an option, I began to understand. Purpose gives you a reason to know why life must go on. (It's ironic that the two poems that seem to deal with this subject best were both written when the poets were in their twenties: Lament and The Love Song of J. Alfred Prufrock. The fact that they understood so young what it took me so long to comprehend is probably a measure of the difference between really smart people and me.)

The other thing that occurred to me, though, is that purpose is a choice. Nobody says that when you're old and have done all the things expected of you in raising a family and earning a living, you can't choose new things to pursue and be passionate about.

The same thing is probably true about the shared purpose that keeps couples heading in the same direction. Years ago I knew a couple who worked very long hours building a business. They worked so hard that it was the subject of some conversation and occasional admiration. After years of this, the business became successful. Shortly after that, the couple divorced. There was a collective shaking of heads; why, after all that work, couldn't they simply enjoy their success together.

I don't really know why, but my guess is that what they shared were the purpose and the struggle. When it was done, they didn't have a lot to hold them together.

If that's true, it was still a matter of choice. If the purpose has been achieved, find a new purpose.

There are some things about growing old that militate against pursuing new purposes. When you're young, all things are possible. When you're old, you've encountered enough grim reality to know that only some things, probably only a few, are possible. Then there's the feeling that you've been there, done that, and it made you tired. You just don't feel like getting that tired again. And there's my personal favorite: what's the use? Given the fact that you have so much more past than you have future, it's not worth worrying about.

But those are all just excuses, born of weariness, fear, or indecision. And that's the conclusion I came to. They're all excuses, and it's not so much a matter of dying with our boots on as it is making sure that our last step is actually going somewhere.

So I'll trade in Edna's lines for some from one of my least favorite poets, William Ernest Henley. Not nearly so good in terms of literature, but probably better to wake up with in the morning:

> *It matters not how strait the gate,*
> *How charged with punishments the scroll,*
> *I am the master of my fate,*
> *I am the captain of my soul.*

Just how good was the Samaritan?

The attacks in Paris and the millions of Syrian refugees have caused a lot of soul searching on social media (which may not be the best place to search your soul, anyway). Some people don't have a lot of problem making a decision, such as the man who said that he "didn't suffer from the moral ambiguity" that caused people to wrestle with what our response should be. His opinion was that any number of their lives didn't equate to the life of a single US serviceman.

Somehow, I couldn't see that his opinion even rose to the level of moral ambiguity. To me the wholesale weighting of lives—one kind of life is more valuable than another—is immoral.

Another poster pulled a verse from 1 Timothy out of context (*But if anyone does not provide for his own, and especially for those of his own house, he has denied the faith and is worse than an unbeliever.*)

However, there are others, some of whom I know to be serious and practicing Christians who are trying to find the Christian balance between compassion and safety. Sometimes they resort to analogy: would you feed grapes to your child if you knew that one percent of them were poisoned, or would you encourage your daughter to pick up hitchhikers? So far, all of the analogies I've seen were seriously flawed, usually because they only dealt with the "fear" side. Nobody was particularly concerned with the fate of the grape or the hitchhiker.

For Christians, there's another story that should give us some insight into WWJD. It's the story of the Good Samaritan. Everybody knows the story; it's a Sunday School staple. A lawyer asks Jesus how to have eternal life. And Jesus answers his question with a question: What is written in the law? How do you read it? The lawyer responds that the law says he should love God and love his neighbor as himself.

Then the lawyer has a lawyerly question: Who is my neighbor?

Jesus answers with the parable of the Good Samaritan. The elevator pitch for the story is simple: A man, traveling from Jerusalem to Jericho is mugged and left in a ditch. A couple of religious officials see him and keep walking. A Samaritan rescues him. However, it goes a lot deeper than the plot outline suggests.

Everyone in the crowd listening to Jesus already knew what the Jews thought of the Samaritans. When the Northern Kingdom fell in the 8th century BC, much of the population was deported. Others were brought in to replace them. So the Samaritans, once as Jewish as the people Jesus was talking to, were mixed blood. To the Jew, the Samaritans were inferior in bloodline and in religion. Forget about a Jew crossing the street to avoid Samaritans; they walked around an entire country. The Jews expected nothing good of Samaritans.

And there were the professional religious people. Jesus gives them no slack at all; he says they saw battered traveler and crossed the road, leaving their bleeding, naked kinsman in the ditch. Then, the Samaritan comes along. He sees the Jew, cleans and bandages his wounds, and takes him to an inn. He gave the innkeeper the equivalent of a couple of days' wages and told him to do what he had to. The Samaritan would take care of it when he came back.

Most of the time when we study the story of the Good Samaritan, we concentrate on the difference between those who profess religion—the Priest and the Levite—and those who practice it. I've never heard anyone go into what to me is the most interesting question: why did Jesus, talking to a congregation of Jews, choose to make the Samaritan the hero? Wouldn't the story about helping your neighbor been just as effective if it had been a Samaritan in the ditch, and a Jew came along and saved him?

I don't know why it's the Good Samaritan rather than the Good Jew, but I have a theory. Just as the Jews despised and looked down on the Samaritans, the Samaritans, logically enough, despised the Jews. If the hero had been a Jew, the congregation could have gathered their self-righteousness around them, convinced themselves that they wouldn't be like the priest or the Levite and gone on their way.

However, Jesus didn't let them off the hook. He said to the lawyer, "Which of the three do you think was a neighbor to the man who fell into the hands of robbers."

I can imagine that the lawyer almost choked on the answer: The one who had mercy on him. He probably couldn't bring himself to simply say, "The Samaritan."

Jesus told the lawyer to go and do likewise. It's not reported whether he did nor not.

So we have the answer to the question, "How good was the Good Samaritan?" The answer is that he's better than we are if weigh the value of life and find others' less valuable than our own, than we are if we can ignore the needs of others because we've determined that their religion is not as authentic as our own, than we are if we interpret "providing for our families" to mean failing to help the helpless. This is "not in my back yard" writ extremely large.

If we are going to be Christians—followers of Christ, living in imitation of Christ—we are commanded to go and do likewise. To me, that means that we have to save others, whether we like them or not. I realize that we can't simply open our borders, but nobody is suggesting that. We currently have a vetting process in place that takes two years. Congress is sending a bill to the president with a provision that would make the vetting process take essentially an eternity. Maybe more.

It is possible that some small percentage of terrorists will be admitted with the refugees. There's a greater possibility that terrorists will enter the country flying coach and passing through customs. The requirements are much more stringent for refugees than for tourists.

Then a purely practical question: Which action will most likely increase our witness, opening the door, however cautiously, or simply slamming it in their face?

Bang! Bang! We're dead.

When I was very young, my dad owned a gun. It wasn't much of a gun, a single-shot twenty-two. Occasionally, late in the afternoon, he'd go down to the trash dump and shoot rats. When I got older—say, four or five—I owned cap pistols (also single-shot) and later a lever-action air rifle.

We played cowboys and Indians and cops and robbers, getting our instruction two days a week at the Princess Theatre and acting it out the rest of the week.

I would imagine most of the families I knew in Benson owned some sort of gun—a rifle, shotgun, or maybe both—and I imagine that most of them used them for hunting or taking care of varmints. The guns were just one of their tools.

And they would no more have gone into town with a gun on their hip than with a Phillips screwdriver. They knew that they would have looked silly.

My point is that I have no problem with people owning guns. However, I do have a real problem with the glorification of guns, the creation of what some people are trying to sell us as a "gun culture."

Before some of my gun-toting friends pipe up with the Second Amendment, I would like to remind them that for most of our lives, the Second Amendment had nothing to do with their right to put a Glock on their hip and go to the mall. It wasn't until DC v. Heller in 2008 that the court held that that the Second Amendment granted an individual right to own and bear arms. Even that opinion said that the right did not extend to all weapons.

The decision prior to that was about Jack Miller's taking a sawed-off shotgun across state lines. In that case (1939), the Court ruled that: "[i]n the absence of any evidence tending to show that possession or use of a [sawed-off] shotgun . . . has some reasonable relationship to the preservation or efficiency of a well-regulated militia, we cannot say that the Second Amendment guarantees the right to keep and bear such an instrument."

But, as with a lot of Supreme Court decisions, the legalities have little to do with our everyday life. People in these United States have owned guns since the nation was founded. However, except for cops and robbers, it did not dictate their identity. People did not place ads in the paper with pictures of their assault rifles.

They knew they would have looked silly.

It appears that we have some sort of perfect storm that causes the minority of our population that owns firearms to have a disproportionate impact on our culture. In no particular order, I think the components of the storm are as follows:

In the Heller decision, the "strict constitutionalist" Anthony Scalia wrote an opinion that not only overturned a couple of centuries of case law but reduced the prefatory clause in the Second Amendment to an "annotation." (However, a part of his ruling that doesn't get mentioned as often is the part that says "the Second Amendment right is not a right to keep and carry any weapon in any manner and for any purpose.") With the Heller ruling, the court confirmed Heller's right to own a handgun and keep it in his home.

The second thing is the Internet. Once upon a time, if you wanted to put your opinion before hundreds or thousands of people, it took some effort. Sometimes it even took some thought.

93

That didn't mean that all opinions were for the public good. Father Coughlin, for instance, fouled up the airwaves for an hour every week from WJR and later from his own radio link-up. He combined religion, anti-Semitism, and a fondness for fascist governments. He found a lot of people who agreed with him.

However, in an age where information flow was limited, Coughlin was an exception. Now, anybody who owns a computer and an internet connection can reach as many people as he did. So we get Facebook posts where people are bragging about their guns and daring "bad guys" to come get them. They are fantasizing about stopping bad guys with their good-guy guns. And we get posts like the Christmas card I saw last week that had a picture of a large family smiling for the camera, each one of them, even the five-year-old, armed. Their version of Peace and Good Will. If I had a nickel for every picture of a large firearm I've seen on the Internet, I could probably buy a legislator.

Finally, our penchant for declaring anyone other than us to be "bad guys." This isn't new. We rounded up the Japanese during World War II, ignoring the German-American Bund who wanted us to enter the war on the side of the Axis Powers. We've hated a lot of people in our history. However, because of item 2 above, we can spread that hate much more efficiently.

Add it up: people who claim that the Supreme Court (specifically DC v. Heller) gives them the right to carry a gun anywhere they want, a constant carnival of opinion (informed and otherwise) that glorifies guns, and what seems to be an insatiable need to declare whole groups of people to be "bad guys." What could possibly go wrong there?

I don't want your guns. I don't want somebody to come get your guns. But I don't want you sitting at the table next to me in the restaurant with a pistol on your hip or an AK-47 propped against the table. You may have been granted that right by the legislature of the State of Georgia, but it doesn't make me feel any safer. Especially since the legislature, maintaining a constancy of intelligence, also says you can't check to see if the gun toter has a permit or is just your average, everyday serial killer.

Fear not! Say what?

When I was teaching Sunday School, I rather dreaded the lessons in the run-up to Christmas. For one thing, I had been teaching the same class for nearly 10 years, and it was tough not to repeat what I had said for the last six, seven, or eight years. After all, everybody knew the story and how it came out.

The second reason may have been more limited to people with strange and twisted senses of humor. Like mine. Somewhere in the three or four weeks before Christmas, we almost always encountered Luke 2. In case age has left a vacancy where you have always stored this particular passage, I'll remind you: it's the narrative of the birth of Christ. I always did fine down through verse 7, but by the time we hit verse 8, I was having trouble keeping a straight face.

I certainly didn't want the class to think that I was finding something funny in the birth of the Savior. However, it does conjure up some strange mental images. Here the story turns from Mary, Joseph, and Jesus and focusses on some shepherds.

I've never met a shepherd, but I can imagine that these were not white collar, executive types. In fact, they worked nights. They were, as the KJV says, "abiding in the field" keeping an eye out on their flock. This is probably something they had done before, and except for the appearance of the odd lion or other scavengers, it probably wasn't very exciting.

"What did you do last night, Daddy?"

"Not much. Just sat in the field and watched the flock."

However, this was a very different night. All of a sudden, there's an angel and what is generally interpreted as a very bright light. Their reaction was predictable. The KJV says that they were "sore afraid." No kidding.

If I were a shepherd sitting on a Galilean hillside minding my own business and somebody else's sheep, and a bright light and an angel appeared, I think I would have been more than "sore afraid." (But even that depicts it better than the more modern translations' "terrified.")

And this is the part where I have difficulty holding it together. I have this mental image of these shepherds, pushing backward so hard they're making a hole in the ground, their eyes about the size of saucers, and wondering if they've just met their Maker. Abject terror. Real sore afraidness.

And the angel says, "Fear not."

In my mind, the bravest of the shepherds looks at him and says, "Say what?"

When suddenly your familiar world is made totally unfamiliar, and you're seeing things that you've not only never seen before, but never really imagined, do you really believe you could just decide to "fear not."

However, the Bible says they did. When the angel had delivered his message, they got up and ran into Bethlehem where they found Mary, Joseph, and the baby Jesus. Then they went out and told everybody.

The fact that I find the mental image funny doesn't mean that I don't take the message seriously. Probably more seriously now than I ever have in my life. Like the shepherds, my familiar world has become much less familiar.

Fifty or sixty years ago there was no such thing as road rage. It's true that you could get your nose broken if you used a term denigrating somebody's mother or called them a liar, but you probably wouldn't get shot.

And people usually, to use my mother's words, "kept a civil tongue in their head," even if they didn't like somebody. And if you were a gentleman you didn't use bad language in front of ladies. But all of that has changed. Civil tongues have become rare, and even people of the female persuasion use bad language, very casually.

But probably the worst thing is that people try to control us using fear. We've gone from "fear not" to "be afraid, very afraid." They tell us that they'll save us from the bad people who are trying to kill us and take what we have from us. All we have to do is give up some of our liberties, sign on to draconian laws, and take out our anger on whole groups of people.

At the moment, Muslims are the target. Last month it was refugees. A couple of months ago it was immigrants. You could build a case against pro-lifers, pro-choicers, the mentally ill, the estranged, and the deranged. It seems that most or all of our politicians want to bomb indiscriminately. Some of our politicians enlist in the 800-year-old strategy of the Abbot of Citeaux, a Papal legate. His army was out hunting heretics (mostly Cathars), and when he was told that his soldiers couldn't really tell the good guys (Catholics) from the bad guys (Cathars), his reported response was (translated from the Latin), "Kill them all, and let God sort them out."

Tis the season to revisit Luke 2:8 and to take that lesson seriously. It's hard to have the joy of the season when we're looking over our shoulder and trying to decide whom to hate or even kill.

We need to take a page out of the shepherds' book and actually fear not. Then go and tell everyone.

My resolutions for what should be the most joyous of seasons are that I will keep a civil tongue in my head; I will watch my language around everybody, and I will value all innocent life as Christ commanded. Or at least I'll do my best.

May each of you have a Merry Christmas full of joy and peace.

Age is…

Have you ever noticed that the people who say that "age is just a number" have an age that's a fairly small number? In other words, they don't know what they're talking about.

There are probably several hundred different ways to finish the sentence "Age is …," some more pessimistic than others and almost none being particularly optimistic. Once you hit sixty-five, it's hard to come up with anything to look forward to when another year passes.

Age is waking up in the morning wondering which joint is not going to work today.

I'm not complaining. I've been given more than my allotted three score and ten, and I'm still upright and taking nourishment. But I know that it's a very short trip from "his mind's as sharp as it ever was" to "doesn't he look natural."

Age is standing at the bottom of the steps wondering if you're about to go up or have just come down.

No matter how optimistic you may be, it's hard to be fearless in the face of aging. Every time you hear of a friend who has to call to get directions back home from downtown or who goes to lunch and can no longer make sense of the menu, you wonder about your own capacities. Not only how quick they may go, but whether they're really as good as you think they are.

Age is laughing in the face of the roofing salesman who asks if you want a twenty-year warranty.

And then there are all the new decisions you have to make with an old mind. At what point do you decide that you need to move into a community of "active seniors," or a facility for not-so-active seniors? When do you decide that the next time your driver's license comes up for renewal, you'll just let it go? Should you take a trip that takes you out of commuting distance to one or more of your doctors?

Those decisions are probably no harder than the ones we made when we bought the house and certainly no harder than the ones we made when we were trying to figure out how to raise the children without doing them bodily or psychological harm. But they seem so final. It's the sort of downsizing that goes way beyond throwing out twenty-year-old magazines.

Age is choking up almost every time you look up an address in your address book because of all of the names crossed out.

However, there are reasons to keep looking forward. Having seen the children grow up to be good people, you get to watch your grandchildren do the same thing. Every winter the collards come in, and every summer the fresh tomatoes. There's always another book that might be interesting and there's a chance for a conversation with another aging individual that goes beyond the well-known "organ recital."

Age is looking into the mirror and wondering if plastic surgery is really all that expensive.

I haven't come to a conclusion is regarding age, and I probably won't. It's not necessary. Every day I still get to make decisions that dictate what kind of person I am. Every day I can still find some way to be useful. And every day I get to see people I love and who love me. And that's not a bad thing at all.

Age is waking up on a whole lot of mornings, putting your feet on the floor, and going to do what needs to be done.

From Church Street to Main Street

In yesterday's AJC there was a picture of a man with a colander on his head. It seems that he's a Pastafarian, and he's claiming that the headdress was a part of his religion. If, he says, other religions are allowed to wear their head coverings (yarmulkes, hijabs) in driver license photographs, he should be able to wear his.

The Pastafarians, as with all religions, have their own creation story, and they have exchanged the 10 Commandments for the 8 I Really Wish You Wouldn'ts.

Now, this guy is at war with the DMV about whether he can wear a colander in his license photo.

Starting new religions isn't a new thing. When I was in college we claimed that the only thing that kept us from starting one was that we couldn't find a virgin to sacrifice. It was all done in good, clean and possibly heretical fun.

However, for people my age, there's another trend in religion that's a lot more serious, another fragmentation of the faith.

In my home town, the first street north of Main is Church Street, so called because four of the town's half-dozen or so churches are on it. Benson Baptist, then the largest in town, sat on one corner. Three blocks away was the Methodist. And a couple of blocks from that were the Pentecostal Church and the Catholic Church.

One street over, on Hill Street, were the Freewill Baptist Church and the Presbyterian Church.

It was all very orderly. You could walk by all of Benson's major religious establishments in less than 10 minutes.

The churches are still there. However, it's a lot like the kindergarten rhyme:

This is the church.

This is the steeple.

Open the door, and where are the people.

The membership of every major denomination is falling, and according to several studies, attendance as a percentage of membership is declining still more. According to one study, the actual "regular" church attendance is about half of what the self-reported studies are showing.

Where did all the people go?

Some of them died. Some just decided to stay home. Some went to megachurches. And some join tiny congregations housed in storefronts on Main Street. Benson has three of them in one block.

It's this group that really interests me.

I know from experience that orthodoxy is a very tricky thing. Some years back, I discovered that my explanation of the Trinity—admittedly convenient and simplistic—had been declared heretical in the fourth century after a hundred years or more of debate. I can't help wonder what the storefront preachers, fervent but not necessarily well-schooled, bring to the Faith. Or even whether the fact that they are not necessarily well-schooled is a good thing or a bad thing.

We don't know what these storefront churches will mean to Christianity in our country. As somebody, maybe Niels Bohr, once said, "Prediction is very difficult, especially about the future."

However, we can look back at the Reformation and see a pattern. Of the churches started during the Reformation, some took root and grew. Some were popular for a while, then disappeared. And some started small and stayed that way. Any of these may be true for the church snuggled between the barber shop and the hair salon.

Whatever their future, in the spirit of brotherly love and having observed what is happening and has happened to organized religion, I have a few suggestions for New Year's Resolutions these churches can have for today. Maybe they are sufficiently baggage-free that they can actually use them.

1. Act like Jesus. It seems that we have gotten so caught up in denominational dogma that we've lost sight of the Biblical Jesus. He didn't have a Recreational Building or a Fellowship Hall. However, he did feed the hungry, heal the sick, shame the proud, and lift up those who were down. In the 2000 edition of the Baptist Faith and Message, the denomination took out the line that said, "The criterion by which the Bible is to be interpreted is Jesus Christ." Maybe one of the storefront churches can put it back in.

2. Don't get horsey about your doctrine. No matter how certain you are that you're right, you'll never make a lot of friends by telling everybody else that they are wrong. Even Saint Paul knew that. When he was preaching at Mars Hill, he acknowledged that the Athenians were "very religious." Then he linked his message to what they already worshipped. If Paul, with all his Pharisaic strictness, could do that, so should we.

3. Remember that what's outside the storefront is more important than what is inside. Some of our churches have gotten so insular that their influence ends at their walls. It's warm and comfortable inside, and it's cold, messy and sometimes full of conflict outside. But that's where Christianity is supposed to operate. A corollary to that is that what we do has more impact than what we say or even what we believe.

4. Be known for who and how you love rather than who and what you hate. When I was young, the Baptists were noted for being "narrow;" that is, we had little tolerance for other opinions. Over the last couple of decades, we've been better known for what we didn't like than what we did, forgetting everything that Jesus and St. John said about loving one another. (I'm not saying that the Baptists are unique in doing this; it's just that I'm Baptist.)

I really don't think God cares whether people worship in a steepled, brick edifice or a storefront. I do think he cares about what we believe and what we do. Otherwise, we might as well wear a colander on our head.

As Needed When Needed

Recently I saw a post on Facebook where the poster said that she'd done everything she had ever done without any help from anybody else. "Nobody gave me anything," she wrote.

That made me sad. If that was indeed true, she had a much rougher time than I did, even though we came from similar circumstances. It seems that every time I needed a hand, somebody was there to provide it. And that's a blessing I am very grateful for.

One of those people was Josefina Niggli, the lady who ran the writing program at Western Carolina. Before Josefina got it, it was called the Journalism program; she renamed it Professional Writing.

By the time I met Josefina in the second quarter of my freshman year I had already been invited out of the Music Department and the Chemistry Department and was rapidly wearing out my welcome in the Math Department. Gary Carden, the editor of the campus literary magazine, lived across the hall from me in the dorm, and for some reason, he asked me if I had anything I wanted to submit. Probably because I was on the staff of the school newspaper.

I submitted a short story which was accepted, and the magazine came out at about the same time the twenty-four-year-old head of the chemistry department asked me what I thought I would ever do with a chemistry degree. Especially since I wasn't very good at it. Since I couldn't give Dr. Squibb a reasonable answer, I started wondering what I would do next.

One afternoon Bob Abbott showed up at my dorm room door and said that Josefina Niggli wanted to see me. I wasn't really sure who she was, had never spoken to her, and hadn't even thought of investigating either English or Writing as majors. When I got to her office, I saw that she had a copy of my story.

"It appears that you might have some talent," she said. "You may enroll in the professional writing program if you want to."

I learned later that the only way you got into Josefina's program was by invitation. If you enrolled without an invitation, she'd ask you to leave. She wasn't in the business of teaching writing; she was in the business of teaching writers how to make a living at it.

In the three and a half years I studied with her, I—and after we were married, Linda and I—became close to Josefina and Mama Niggli, and we learned a lot about her rather strange background.

Josefina's father was an engineer, and her mother was a concert violinist. She was raised in Mexico and educated there in a German convent. She sold her first story in English when she was sixteen. She was fluent in English, Spanish, and German, and sometimes didn't seem sure which language she was speaking. (One of my jobs in college was to sit right in front of her desk and signal her when she lapsed into Spanish or was about to put the wrong end of her Marlboro in her mouth. She paid me in Marlboros.)

She wrote a novel entitled *Step Down, Elder Brother* (made into a movie starring Ricardo Montalban and Cyd Charisse) that got her a spot in a Hollywood studio's stable of writers. Then she went to UNC at Chapel Hill (where she became friends with Betty Smith) and finally to Western Carolina.

She was a professional writer, having sold novels, screenplays, poems, and articles. Her purpose in the Western Carolina program was to help somebody else do that. But she went a lot further than the position required. Her office door was open to us, her

107

home was open to us, and she spoke kindly to us when it was needed. And she was brutal when she critiqued our writing. She taught us to do the same thing.

She didn't teach me to write. She contended that nobody could do that, and I agree with her. But she did take a real interest in me, along with a number of others, and helped us believe that we could write something worthwhile without having to starve to do it. For years after I left Western Carolina, I would send her ads, brochures, and scripts that I had written. She always marked them up and responded, not to change those pieces, but to help me do better next time.

Josefina was just one of a lot of people who came into my life when I needed them. For those people who feel that they've never been given anything, I wish I could share. I've been given more than I deserve.

Earning a Valentine

A couple of weeks ago Linda and I were having lunch with my ex-partner (and one of my older—in several ways— friends) and his wife. Between us, we had something over 100 years of married life and we had all gone through almost all of the marriage vows—better, worse, richer, poorer, sickness, health. And we're well on our way to the "until death do you part" one.

I thought about this as I was watching yet another Valentine's movie the other night. They all have essentially the same plot: the lead hates Valentine's Day because of a failed romance. He or she runs into someone who through thoughtfulness, good looks, and active hormones changes his or her mind about it, and after a couple of bumps in the road, they go off to happy-everafterness. Valentine's wins again.

But if that's the sort of thing Valentine's is intended to celebrate, it's not a lot more meaningful than the Valentines cards that we got in the second grade. You know the deal: everybody brought a Valentine for everybody else. Sort of like a trophy for participation.

I think that's great for seven-year-olds, but for adults, I think there should be some requirements for Valentining. Sort of like the requirements for a Purple Heart. For people who don't meet these requirements, there could be various levels of apprentice Valentineship leading up to full-fledged Valentine.

The first requirement that I would propose is tenure. Nobody should ask anybody to commit to being his or her Valentine until they've been together for at least 10 years. That period could be reduced if the number of resulting children exceeds 2. But it should be increased if one or both parties spend a lot of time on the road or apart for any other reason (such as voluntary separation). I suppose an argument could be made for five years, but I've known people who could be blissfully ignorant longer than that.

The second criterion should be experience. I'm not sure that you can tell whether anybody's really your Valentine unless you have been through one or more serious illnesses (something more life-threatening than snoring). It's these times, when one of you is down and essentially helpless, that tears any veneer from the surface of a relationship and gets down to its core. I think it's essential that we can accept the other's weakness as well as their strength, their helplessness as well as their helpfulness.

An alternative to the really sick thing might be going through difficult financial straits. Hard financial times really clarify a relationship. You learn whether you or the other person is more interested in things such as status and keeping up with whomever than in the relationship. You also learn how the other deals with disappointment. (I suppose one of the advantages of getting married when you're young, don't have anything and don't know whether you'll ever have anything is that it keeps the expectations low. I have always been grateful for low expectations.)

I think that anyone who has lived through these things and still wants to get up and give the other one a good morning kiss qualifies as a Valentine, more or less worthy of the saint for which the day was named. (For those of you without Google, St. Valentine was a Roman priest who encouraged Romans to marry within the Christian church. This was counter to the edicts of Claudius II, and for that, Valentine was jailed, beaten, and eventually executed. I'm not sure how that got to a frilly card and a box of chocolates, but Hallmark could probably tell us.)

To those who meet the criteria, a very happy Valentine's Day and another year of togetherness, love, and forbearance. To those who don't, continue to aspire. As my mother always said, if a job's worth doing, it's worth doing well.

And to my Valentine, may our years keep getting better until, as we vowed, death do us part.

A Life in Four Phrases

Being a person who has strange and random thoughts has its advantages and disadvantages. The primary advantage is that it's a cheap and portable form of entertainment, sometimes causing you to laugh out loud in a solemn place like the line at the DMV. The disadvantage is that it sometimes causes you to laugh out loud in solemn places, causing people to wonder, quite correctly, if you're weird.

While stuck in an unmoving line the other day I had one of those random thoughts: lives can generally be summarized by four phrases. But further thought led me to believe that this was, at best, an imperfect model. Maybe even wrong.

First the four phrases.

We start off with, "Isn't he (she) cute." This one is reserved for newborns and other small children. It seems like the sight of a baby will cause any woman's heart to melt, no matter what the baby looks like. My mother, who occasionally made bassinets—little, bitty, frilly beds—for expectant mothers, would go completely out of character when faced with a baby. "Isn't she (he) cute." Sometimes she would add, "Just darling."

I should note here that this is what she said even when the baby looked like a very small eighty-year-old man who had been parboiled. Bald. Wrinkled. And with a rosy red complexion.

I should note, too, that the subject of all this gushing really didn't have any responsibility for it. All the baby did was get born.

The second phrase comes along anywhere from 18 to 38 years later. It's "he's such a promising young man." This or its female variant is generally said of anyone who's found gainful employment, managed to keep it, and has stayed out of jail. Other than that, it's applied pretty indiscriminately. When I was young there were "promising young men" all over the place. Some of them did something. Some didn't; they simply stopped being young.

Then we skip down about forty or so years, and we hear, "His mind's as sharp as it ever was." For the most part, this means that the subject doesn't drool a lot or still does crossword puzzles or manages to match up subjects and verbs correctly. There's not a very high standard for it.

In fact, there's a pretty low standard. For most of our life, we are encouraged to try to get better every day. Then we reach the point where it's remarkable that we haven't gotten worse. That's depressing.

Finally, there's "doesn't he look natural." Again, this doesn't really have much to do with the subject. It means that the Undertaker has done a pretty good job. If I am ever laid out in a casket (and given my post-parting instructions, that's doubtful), this phrase will probably be roughly equivalent to, "They finally got all five of the cowlicks to lay down at the same time."

So we go from cute to natural in a short span of years. We don't know anything when we're cute, and we know less when we're natural. And when we're promising, it's not a lot our fault.

Which led me to the flaw in this whole thing. There's a significant span called middle age when we do know something, when we're really doing something, and when we either shoulder our responsibilities or don't. There's no appropriate phrase that goes along with it.

There is, of course, talk of midlife crisis, but that simply describes a degree of psychosis that men (and probably women, although they call it something else) go through when they discover that they've got as much time behind them as they have in front of them, and they're not half-way to the goal line. People have quit calling them promising young men.

These are the years where working people have either gotten far enough up the corporate ladder that their responsibilities significantly exceed their authority, or they've come to the conclusion that they're never going to go as far as they had hoped, planned, and expected. In some cases, especially with people who have chosen to make their own way as artists, musicians, writers, or entrepreneurs, this is the time when they become good enough to know that they will never become good enough to achieve the dream they originally started chasing.

And these are the years when their children not only learn that their parents aren't infallible, they remind them of it several times a day. The child in the bassinet that you stood over just to make sure you could hear his or her breath has become a teenager, and you wonder if the entire concept of children shouldn't be revisited.

These are also the years when your parents have grown old, and you worry about your responsibilities to them, and whether you should make decisions for the same people who spent so many years making decisions for you.

These are the years when the world seems to be upside down: the people you took care of don't want you to take care of them anymore and the people who took care of you need your care.

It's a bewildering time.

But we don't have a good phrase for it. Somehow "isn't he responsible" really doesn't have the cachet. I've heard people say that someone is "a good provider," but that essentially reduces the person to an ATM. I'm really at a loss for the defining phrase.

Probably it's not something I should worry a lot about. I'm no longer cute (if I ever was, but my mother thought so). I am no longer promising. I am, I think, as sharp as I ever was, but it seems to be a bit of a rear-guard action. And I'm not yet looking natural. I just hope that there are younger, more enthusiastic heads out there who can come up with a good phrase for that time of life when we carry the greatest number of burdens and face the flickering light of our future.

I told you that having random thoughts had its disadvantages.

Slogan Substitution

I find that Facebook is a wonderful source of adrenalin-inducing anger, laughter, and the occasional "SAY WHAT?!" I encountered the latter last week when a Facebook friend who is my age posted one of those "if you (fill in your own cause, belief, or threat here), share this" memes. This particular one had to do with the Pledge of Allegiance.

"Share if you want to keep saying the Pledge of Allegiance like we did when we were children." He was, of course, referring to the phrase "Under God."

Unless his childhood began after he entered high school, this argument has about as much validity as the (probably apocryphal) argument for the King James Bible: it was good enough for Jesus, and it's good enough for me.

The phrase "Under God" was inserted into the Pledge of Allegiance in 1954, changing the 62-year-old pledge. A few years later (1957) we started putting "In God We Trust" on our paper money.

(There are a couple of ironies here. The Pledge of Allegiance was written by a socialist, and the first use of "In God We Trust" on coins was during the civil war, and it's said that at least part of the reason was to emphasize that God was on the Union side.)

I really don't mind saying "under God" in the Pledge, nor am I particularly opposed to having "In God We Trust" on my money (even though E Pluribus Unum does, I think, speak more to where we came from). However, I am upset by the thinking behind both of those additions.

They came from the Cold War, some politician's idea of what it would take to set the United States apart from Godless Communism. If we wanted to be different from that bunch of atheists over there, we had to slap a slogan on something. This was the same era that gave us Joseph McCarthy and the House Un-American Activities committee, guilt by association and blacklisting.

We proudly adopted our slogans, and we've kept on doing it for these sixty-plus years. To me, it's troublesome that people don't seem to question whether adopting a slogan or inserting a couple of the words into the pledge is really useful in terms of showing other people that our people (at least some of them) believe in God. (Another interesting tidbit: Christianity, Judaism, and Islam all have their phrase for "In God We Trust." And unless you teach at certain small colleges you can safely contend that they're talking about the same God.)

I would suggest that if we really want to show the world that we trust in God we quit trying to substitute slogans for actions. Instead of calling for indiscriminate carpet bombing, let's go back to basics:

For I was hungry and you gave me something to eat, I was thirsty and you gave me something to drink, I was a stranger and you invited me in, I needed clothes and you clothed me, I was sick and you looked after me, I was in prison and you came to visit me.

That, of course, is the separation of the sheep from the goats. Doesn't say a word about passing Religious Freedom laws to protect pastors from a problem they don't really have. Doesn't say a thing about banning, prohibiting, or pushing away. Not a syllable about putting us above another. None of the easy things.

It seems that, at least at the political level, we've decided that we can substitute a slogan for actually doing anything. Else how could the Georgia legislature spend all that time on multiple religious freedom bills and no time at all on the twenty percent of our children who are (in the sanitized bureaucratic lexicon) "nutritionally insecure?" How can we, who have been given so much, ignore the needy, the mentally ill, and those who are simply trying to save their and their families' lives? It seems that the most important thing is to have a good slogan and protect people from the somewhat distant eventuality that they may have to associate with those they call sinners. There's a place in the Bible that talks about that, too

Not Under My Bed Or In My Closet

When I was very young, during the war that wasn't supposed to be (since we had already fought the war to end all wars), we had blackout drills. We would pull the shades, turn all the lights off, and wait to be told that we could turn the lights back on again.

I was too young to wonder why. Benson, NC is about 125 miles inland; so, no German subs were going to lob a shell into Medlin & Dorman. And it was too far for German bombers to fly. And if they could, why would they? But we regularly did our blackout drills.

When I wondered about it later, I thought that it might have been to make the war more real to us so that we would keep stomping tin cans and bringing scrap metal in. But nothing could make the war more real than knowing that my daddy wasn't coming home at night and watching my mother sit on the edge of the bed crying. Still later, I finally figured out why a little town a long way from the guns had blackout drills: they—the people who ordered the blackout drills—wanted us to believe that they—the Huns and the Yellow Hordes—were coming after us.

They stuck a monster under our beds so we would be appropriately and effectively afraid.

Less than ten years after the end of WWII, Collier's ran a photorealistic illustration of Manhattan ablaze under a mushroom cloud. Since we had taken care of the first monster, we needed another. Because of things like that I would stand on the front porch facing what I thought was the northwest, waiting for the missiles that were surely coming from Russia. Than monster lasted a long time.

It seems important to people who want to direct us that we be properly afraid.

In my lifetime I've been told that I should fear Jews, Catholics, Blacks, Yankees, Gays, Mexicans, poor people, rich people, religious people, atheists (or secular humanists), Japanese, Germans, Muslims, Communists and probably two or three other groups that I've forgotten. All of these people were intent on taking something important away from me. At least, that's what I was told.

Everybody has somebody they want me to be afraid of. Because if I'm sufficiently afraid, I can be stampeded into doing very strange things and believing even stranger ones.

For instance, otherwise rational people in Germany were convinced that the Jews were going to destroy their country and had to be stopped. This at a time when the Jewish population of Germany was less than 1% of the total.

We got so fearful of the Japanese that we rounded up thousands of them, took their property, and put them into camps. Even though they were US citizens and had committed no crime except that of being of Japanese extraction.

We have people calling us to arms to defend our religion against the war on Christianity. Even though about 70% of the people in the US identify themselves as Christians. And much of this seems to be based on whether a store clerk that I don't know wishes me "Happy Holidays," instead of "Merry Christmas."

And this month a person who was presumably considered sane by his constituents when they elected him to the Georgia legislature proclaimed that he was going to introduce the "Pastor's Protection Act," to keep pastors from having to choose between following their religious convictions and performing same-sex marriages. He must not have gotten the memo that pastors can—and have—refused to perform marriages for a number of reasons. Some won't marry people who have been divorced. Some won't marry people of different races. Some won't marry people of different faiths. The preacher who performed my daughter's wedding would not marry a couple unless they completed a series of premarital sessions.

Since the legislator seems to be protecting people who don't really need his protection, I would refer him to a group that does: the 20% of Georgia children who are—in bureaucratese—nutritionally insecure. That means they are hungry. Work on that for a while.

There are things we should deal with. September 11 taught us that, but we should deal with them specifically. After September 11 I thought that we should pursue with all of our might the people who had attacked us on our own soil. Instead, we invaded Iraq.

I am not a pacifist. In fact, I am a proponent of disproportionate retaliation. And we do have real enemies that we have to deal with. But I'm very much for making sure we aim at the right targets and use the right weapons. I will not let anybody convince me that allowing two men or two women to get married is going to make my own marriage a bit less holy. Nor am I going to let terrorists such as the coward who gunned down the four Marines in Tennessee this week be used as a reason to convince me that we should go invade another country.

I'm just tired of people or groups of people trying to turn my fear into their profit. And I'm just as tired of people who enlist in these phony wars. I will make it a point to treat Jews, Catholics, Blacks, Yankees, Gays, Mexicans, poor people, rich people, Japanese, Germans, Muslims, and—if I should ever encounter one—communists not with tolerance, because they should not have to wait for me to tolerate them, but with respect. Because I genuinely believe that most people out there really don't want to take anything important away from me.

No monsters. Not under my bed or in my closet.

Looking for God in all the Big Places

On page 92 of his book, *Stars Beneath Us*, Paul Wallace writes about learning something he already knew—a second learning, as it were. I experienced that as I was reading his book: Wallace articulates—and does it well—something I had only been able to intuit.

Of course, Paul Wallace has an advantage; he's far better educated, holding a Ph.D. in experimental nuclear physics and a Masters of Divinity. He's both a scientist and a cleric, a combination that gives him a particular, if not unique, view of the world that God made.

And it's a view that might upset a lot of people who call themselves religious but insist on creating God in their own image.

I can sympathize with this. About twenty-five years ago, I was teaching a college-age Sunday School class and was cautioning them against the popular image of a "vending machine God:" deposit a prayer and watch an answer fall into the tray below. One of my favorite class members (because he had a smart mouth that didn't seem to have a switch on it) asked, "Then why do you worship God?" My answer was quick and probably without the benefit of ratiocination: "Because God is God, and I'm not."

Quick and thoughtless as it may have been, I've held to that concept ever since. I worship a God so great and powerful that if He chooses to ignore me, I still cannot ignore Him.

And that's the reason that Job is probably my favorite book in the Bible, the same reason that it forms the spine of Stars Beneath Us. Job, at least for most of the book, upends the traditional worship-reward model of Man-God relationship.

It's not that I like reading about the suffering Job: loss, death, and boils. I do always get a chuckle at the first interchange between God and Satan. In my head, they sound like a couple of homeboys:

GOD: Yo, Satan, where you been?

SATAN: Just roamin' to and fro across the Earth.

Then comes what might be the most incomprehensible sentence in the entire Bible: Hast thou considered my servant Job?

God, without reason or provocation, fingers Job, whom he calls "a perfect and upright man," and sets in motion the destruction of Job's very privileged world.

It's great drama, which is probably the reason it's been the basis for several plays, and we see a lot of humanity that we recognize, especially Job's friends, who try to reconcile his troubles with their view of God.

But the part I like best is where Job challenges God, and God responds (very loose paraphrase): Sit down and shut up, Job. I'm God and you're not. Then he takes Job on a tour of creation.

All of that I've known for years, but the new perspective that Paul Wallace gave me was that God showed Job a lot of his creation that he was very pleased with that was not human-centric. He seemed to be showing Job that humankind was a part of his creation, but not all of it. Perhaps not even the best of it. And it's the realization that we're simply creatures that gives us an idea of the majesty of God.

Wallace, who is a professor of physics and astronomy at Agnes Scott, devotes a chapter to the idea that in a cosmos as large as we know, there could be other life. He discusses the "six numbers" that have to be calibrated exactly for life to exist, numbers that make life on other planets extremely unlikely, but given the number of other planets, certainly not impossible. They would be God's creation, too.

Several years ago, a Jewish friend of mine called and asked me if it would shake my faith if science discovered life on other planets. He had just received a lecture from a mutual acquaintance who had been converted to the Baptist denomination. I told him it would probably scare me, but it wouldn't shake my faith since I believed that God was free, and if He wanted to create other life, that was His business.

I had gotten over the idea that what I was or what I did was a reason for God to favor me. There was a time that I might have sat on the ash heap with Job, proclaiming my worthiness and claiming the unfairness of my position.

"I am straight. I am white. I teach Sunday School. I passed Dr. Agnes Stout's Advanced Grammar class. I'm a good person, and I don't deserve this."

And God says, "You're looking in all the wrong places."

Wallace and I do have some things in common. He's a member and Sunday School teacher at First Baptist Church Decatur. Linda and I went there for a while. But the most striking commonality is that we both had the same experience a couple of decades apart.

Reverend Bill Self, the pastor of Wieuca Road Baptist, had a formulaic ending to the Sunday Evening service. "It's been a good day," he would say, and then enumerate the reasons it had been a good day. Wallace, as a child, heard that and wondered, because on that "good day" he had witnessed a woman being struck and killed by a bus.

I remember sitting in church and having the same reaction. Earlier in the week, I had spent several hours trying to help one of the kids in the class that I taught understand why his mother left the dinner table, walked into the bathroom, and shot herself in the head. He didn't understand why. Neither did I.

We knew that, contrary to Bill's pronouncement, days weren't good for everybody. Some were downright terrible. But that didn't change who God was, nor did it change our relationship to Him.

I appreciate Paul Wallace's writing this book, and I recommend it to anyone who is interested in being shaken from their sometimes thought-free acceptance of their relationship with God and Jesus. The book is available from Fortress Press (fortresspress.com).

I also appreciate his helping me revisit Job. It reminded me that I really do have the patience of Job, that is, almost none at all.

So this is how history is written.

Bill Sammon begins his book *Misunderestimated* with George W. Bush staring out of his limousine at "a thousand angry demonstrators—maybe more—rampaging through the streets of Portland, Oregon." He depicts the police as losing control of the situation, the president's life as being in danger, and the crowd "seething with hatred."

For the twenty-four pages that he describes the incident, it's the "commander-in-chief," and his polite, well-dressed guests (he was in Portland for a fundraiser) against the hordes in "T-shirts and jeans, do-rags, and dreadlocks."

Eventually, according to Sammon, everybody made it into the fundraiser, the unruly mob dispersed, and having paid $2,000 just to attend plus $25,000 to have their picture taken with the president, we may suppose that everybody had a good time.

The last line of the chapter is full of foreboding. "The president didn't know it as he gazed out the window of his limousine, but he had just caught a glimpse of the Next Big Thing in politics: the rise of the Bush haters." (Sammon must have forgotten that there were protests at George W. Bush's inauguration.)

It may have happened that way, but we'll never know based on Sammon's book. He reports everything as if he were an eyewitness, without attribution, and his book contains no notes.

We do know that there were other points-of-view. One news story, admittedly from the far left, is headlined "Police attack anti-Bush demonstrators in Portland." It reports nearly unrestrained police violence on the protesters, bystanders, and media covering the protests. Later several people sued and collected damages from the police actions.

My problem is that, just as some people would dismiss the leftist news story because it comes from a Socialist Web Site, I am very skeptical of Sammon's version because he is a Bush true believer who almost chokes on verbs and adverbs as he characterizes the Republicans as good, loyal Americans and pretty much everybody else as either weak, disloyal, or not very bright. In his book, Bush "thunders," and the UN Secretary General "tut-tuts," although it must be difficult to talk while tut-tutting. Also, Howard Dean "harrumphed," also a difficult way to talk.

I read a lot of history, especially political history, and I know every book has a point of view, some more slanted than others. However, I shudder to think that some years from now a high school student will use a book like Sammon's as a source for a research paper. In this book, George W. Bush wisely refuses to invade Iraq until he has won the war in Afghanistan (despite the fact that US fatalities in Afghanistan were higher every year after the invasion of Iraq than they were before the invasion). And they'll learn that Secretary of State Colin Powell demanded and received unassailable proof before he went before the UN to put the US's case to the world, but doesn't note—because the book was written in 2004—that Powell called the speech a lasting blot on his record in 2005.

Sammon also gives a play-by-play of the president's 30-minute fly-out to the Lincoln for the Mission Accomplished speech, even though there were eight people on the two planes, and he wasn't one of them. We see the president taking the stick and flying in formation with the other plane (at that point being piloted by Andy Card, who had no pilot training). We see him humbly handing the stick back for the carrier landing. And when he gets out of the plane, we hear his pilot thanking him for "bringing grace and dignity back to the White House."

I won't pretend that I expected to agree with Sammon when I checked the book out of the library. I won't even claim that I approached it with an open mind. I'm one the minority that became a majority (US citizens who think that the invasion of Iraq was a really bad idea). I'm one of the people disgusted with Rumsfeld's dismissive response regarding the fact that soldiers in Iraq were being injured because the vehicles weren't properly armored (You know you go to war with the army you've got, etc.). I'm also one of those English majors who cringed when the leader of the free world invented words like "misunderestimated." But that's not what this is about.

The point is that it seems as if our history is being written by those on the political edges with little regard for truth or accuracy. This isn't a new thing; in the 19th century each of the political parties had its own paper, and that paper's job was to praise its candidates and slam its opponents. However, they were openly partisan. Unlike the partisan papers, this book—and dozens of others on both sides of the political spectrum—attempts to cleverly disguise itself as a serious study of the subject.

I'm sure Sammon is familiar with the concept of attribution; he was the Washington Times Senior White House Correspondent, and he has since been Fox's Washington Bureau Chief. I'm sure he knows better. But for the sake of all those future high school students who might be trying to understand the United States in the years between 2002 and 2004 I just wish he had done better.

Why Some Humans Are Luckier Than Tortoises

Over the years I've encountered a lot of information about mating habits. I know, for instance, that mountain goat males literally butt heads to see whom Miss Mountain Goat goes home with. Strongest mountain goat wins.

Then there's the blue peacock who struts and fans his tail feathers to attract his chosen peahen. If the exhibition impresses her sufficiently, she chooses him back.

And the bird that brings his intended home to check out the nest he's built. She looks it over, and if it's better than the other offers she's had, she moves in.

Or the Galapagos tortoise males who stand as tall as they can and stretch their necks as far as they can. The tallest one wins the female.

Evidently, in order to perpetuate the species, nature has caused the desirable female to choose the biggest, strongest, best looking and most prosperous.

Which makes me wonder how I ever got married. I can only believe that Linda saw something in me that I didn't see or thought she saw something that I didn't really have. Either way, she agreed to marry me. In the fifty-six years we've been man and wife (longer than my relationship with anyone else, relative or otherwise), she has helped shape my life, not in the least by having (with some help from me) two children.

That's the reason that I'm dedicating my Mother's Day blog to Linda instead of to my own mother, who also had a tremendous influence on my life.

If you're a thoughtful person or don't sleep well at night, you may have pondered what might have happened if you had chosen the path not taken at the dozens of different points that you encountered forks in the road. It is, of course, pure speculation, but some speculations are based on more evidence than others.

For instance, if Linda had gone for somebody with more spectacular tail feathers, I believe my adult life would have been much more like my college life, with spotty accomplishments surrounded by big puddles of bad calculations. Marriage and her counsel made me a more dependable person.

And it wasn't long after marriage—eleven months—that we became parents and began learning a whole new role. Together we raised two children—Chuck and Leslie—at times with more skill than at other times. But both of them grew up to be good people who married good people; so I figure that on balance Linda and I did a good job.

So this is for the mother of our children. Together we created a gene pool, a nest, and environment that sent two more into the world. A matter in which we can both take some pride.

I'm glad that you chose me. And I'm glad that we aren't mountain goats, blue peacocks, or Galapagos tortoises. I'd have lost for sure, and I wouldn't be able to wish you a very happy Mother's Day.

$\mathcal{E}$

What makes a man?

If Dad were alive now, he would be 105 next Monday. And he would have hated it.

My father was a peaceable man, mild in all things except for his war against aging. He stopped counting birthdays at 39 and died just short of the 25th anniversary of his 39th birthday. And he fought a good fight. For most of his life, he had jet black hair and weighed within a pound of 153.

He got a particular kick out of being taken for my brother, even though he was 28 years older than I was.

Old was not a destination that Dad looked forward to. And by today's standards, it's not a destination he reached. Two heart attacks in two days took care of that.

I've often wondered what he would have said about the time he did have here. It would have depended, I suppose, on what part of it he was talking about.

In some ways, Dad lived a life of strange circumstances and near misses. He spent four years in the US Navy, and the largest watercraft he was on was the Chesapeake ferry. The Navy trained him to be an airplane mechanic, and I would imagine that he was a good one. But then they decided he would make a good tail gunner. When he finished his training and got his orders to go overseas, the war ended, and he got discharged instead. Although he talked about his time in the Navy, he didn't say whether he liked it or not. That wasn't really much of a consideration. We were at war. He got drafted. Nobody asked him whether he liked it. That was a lesson he took to a lot of things.

Another big part of his life was sports. Dad was a good athlete. Coach Vann recruited him to play on the Benson High School football team, evidently forgetting that Daddy was no longer a student there. He had to do it in secret since grandmother forbade it. The news got out when Daddy came home with a broken hand. I still haven't figured out how anybody plays in a football game secretly.

He played baseball for the Benson Bulls, and I don't think I ever saw him happier than when he was playing. When he couldn't play baseball anymore, he played softball. And when he couldn't play softball, he spent most Sundays watching ball games.

Sports was something that made sense to dad. Using skills. Following rules. Accomplishing things. Winning or losing. In his worldview, it was fairly easy to keep score.

And, as with most men, there was the job. Daddy didn't particularly like his job, but I doubt he ever expected to. It was work. It was a paycheck. It was what a man did, especially one who grew up during the Depression. He was an appliance serviceman, and he was good at it; so good that he would occasionally get offers from other Frigidaire dealers who wanted somebody of his skills to head up their service department. Sometimes they offered him significantly more money than he was making, but he would never take the job. That would have meant leaving Benson.

Which was another important part of his life.

People who grow up in small towns with essentially static populations won't have any trouble understanding the tie he felt to Benson. The family had been there since before the Revolution, and—of the 10 Holmes children—eight of them lived in

Benson. His identity was tied as closely to the town as it was to the family—or even the baseball team. There is a literal connection to the past in Benson, and even as old as I am, if I encounter someone older in Benson, I'm Ed Holmes' boy.

If he was talking about his family, especially my brothers and me, he may have had some difficulty knowing just what to say. It was the opposite of the ordered world of sports. Dad had dreams for his sons: that they would be good athletes and that they would pursue a professional degree that would guarantee a good living. Instead, he got athletes who were somewhat less than good, although my brother Pat may have been a seasonal exception. He was, I'm told, a pretty good fullback on the high school football team.

So far as our professional careers are concerned, two of us majored in English and one majored in Art. Daddy just shook his head. I remember a conversation at Thanksgiving dinner one year.

Ray: I just changed my major to sculpture.

Daddy: How do you make a living as a sculptor.

Ray: You don't.

Even though none of us became engineers, we did learn to make a living. I think he would have been proud of that.

When he was in the Navy, one of his friends said, "You don't drink. You don't smoke. You don't curse. What makes you smell like a man?"

Daddy told that story with no attempt to answer the question. He didn't drink. He didn't smoke. And I heard him curse once. Somebody pulled out in front of us on highway 301. Dad swerved to avoid him, and we started doing 360s on a busy highway. We finally came to rest on the shoulder.

He put his head on the steering wheel, and I heard him mutter, "Son of a bitch." In a very soft voice.

It's almost Father's Day, and because Dad's birthday was always within a few days of Father's Day, he only got one gift, usually a shirt, for both occasions. It's sort of a minor league version of being born on Christmas Day. So, for this Father's Day, I'm going to answer the sailor's question.

For dad, being a man wasn't a matter of smoking, drinking, or cursing. It wasn't a matter of hunting, fishing, or fighting. It was far more important than any of that.

It was a matter of honor, of following the rules, accomplishing things, winning when you could and accepting defeat when you had to. It was a matter of doing what you were supposed to do—hold a job, take care of your family, and never bring shame on your family name.

I suppose it's an archaic definition of manhood, going back to something like chivalry, but it's an honest definition, dealing with things more important than some of the things we consider "manly" today. And by that definition, he was far more of a man than most.

For Richer or What???

Last night Linda and I went out to celebrate our 56th anniversary. We celebrated the fact that we had not only grown old together but grown up together. We talked about a lot of things that happened a long time ago and looked at our wedding pictures. We also appreciated the fact that Tucker, not exactly a culinary capital, had a new restaurant where the food was outstanding.

In all, it was a celebration that wasn't important to anyone but Linda and me and probably to our children. But it was a cause to pause and reflect.

When I told someone we were about to have our 56th anniversary, he said, "That's great. Married to the same woman for 56 years."

And that's where he was wrong. Not about it being great. It is. But not the same woman. Over our married life, I've been married to three or four different women, and Linda has been married to three or four different men.

That's probably a good thing. I can't believe that Linda would want to live for this many years with the naïve, head-full-of-dreams man that she married. What's attractive at 21 is very strange more than half a century later, much like some of the rockers we see still touring into their dotage.

I can't pinpoint the times I went from one person to another. It's a gradual process. There are, of course, markers. Like the week

I bought a sports car and a sailboat. I knew I was trying to stave off middle age, but it came anyway. Then it went.

I think the problem that hurts many marriages may well be that the partners don't understand this.

"You're not the man (woman) I married," she (he) yells.

And the correct response should be: "And you should be very happy for that."

In any long marriage, there are probably good times and bad times. I think the good times are when the partners are in sync, when their concurrent changes hit a harmonious spot. Conversely, the bad times are when the points in the change process are out of sync. The thing to remember is that, since the change process, is continuous, what you need to do is hang on. The synchronization will come again.

There are, however, basics that should be observed, no matter what point the marriage is at.

Doing thoughtful things is important. It may be easier if you're young and hormonal, but it's probably more important when each partner is dealing with the pain of growing older.

Being respectful of each of other is important no matter where in the marriage spectrum you are. If you love someone, you care about what they think, what they say, and how they act toward you. Disrespect tears that down.

Romance is important at the beginning and toward the end, although the definition changes along the way. For instance, I'm sure that my getting Linda's car inspected was more romantic than yet another bunch of flowers or box of chocolates. Romance ceases to be flames and becomes nice warm embers. Maybe not as impressive, but much more enduring.

In 56 years, there are things that we treasure and things we'd sooner forget. But that's real life. That's the reason we vowed for better or for worse, for richer or for poorer, in sickness and in health. In our married life, we've dealt with every one of those things, and last night we were sitting in a somewhat too noisy restaurant eating very good food and remembering the parts that we wanted to.

That, in itself, is worth celebrating. 'Til death do we part.

Living in an Alternate Reality

I hope that there is such a thing as an alternate reality, a reality where it makes sense to repeal Glass-Steagall, to cut the taxes for the richest, and to keep the minimum wage as low as possible because raising it might cut jobs. I hope that there is such a reality because none of those things make sense in this one.

Much of what has passed for economic thought in the last twenty years is no more than magical thinking, based on the idea that if we make the rich very rich, some of it will trickle down to the poor people. And that if we remove regulation, the market will take care of itself.

However, our reality is that the invisible hand of the market just slapped us up beside the head.

Take the Glass-Steagall act. It was created in 1933 by Carter Glass (Senator and founder of the US Federal Reserve System) and Henry Bascom Steagall (chairman of the House Banking and Currency Committee) and it made banks choose whether they would be commercial banks or investment banks. The idea was that highly speculative investments wouldn't take the commercial banks down. FDIC was an amendment to this act.

In 1999, Congress repealed Glass-Steagall and passed the Gramm-Leach-Bliley Act, which knocked down the walls that Glass-Steagall had created.

In doing that, it separated the people who originated mortgages from those who owned them (and cared about whether the payments were made or not).

In 1965, when we bought our first house, we went to Decatur Federal and were grilled by a loan officer. He was very interested in whether we could make the payments. Forty years later, there were thousands of mortgage originators whose compensation was based on getting people to take out a mortgage whether they could make the payments or not. What followed should not have been a surprise.

Most businesspeople know that employees will do what they are paid to do. Pay them a salary if they show up, they show up. Pay them to generate the maximum number of mortgages, and they do that.

It would have been different if the companies who made the mortgages depended on the mortgage payments for their profits.

Or take the argument for lowering the top marginal tax rates, a staple in the Republican platform for years. But we already did that. Today's top marginal tax rate is the lowest it's been since the beginning of the great depression, and it's only about a third of what it once was. Even the IRS knows that if the very rich pay that rate on all of their income, they need to fire their tax accountant. Some of the very rich, because of their friends in Congress, pay much less than the very middle class.

How does that affect our country's economy? If you look at our modern history, for the top 20 years of our country's GDP growth, the lowest top marginal rate was 60%. Of course, several of those years were during the depression when government spending accelerated the growth and several were during WWII. However, if you look at just the 1950s and 1960s, the growth was between 5.6% and 7.3%.

When Reagan was elected president in 1981, the top marginal rate was 70%. When he left in 1989, it was 28%. That was supposed to make the economy blossom. At the beginning of 1981, the GDP growth was 9.62. At the end of 1989, it was 6.48, and except for the Clinton years, it's seldom been that good again. On the average growth was greater with a 90% top marginal rate than with the lower ones.

All of that really doesn't prove that increasing the top marginal rate would make the economy grow, but it pretty well disproves that lowering it will.

And, finally, the minimum wage. Adjusted for inflation, a minimum wage worker today is making about 70% of what a minimum wage worker was making in 1968. And the current minimum wage ($7.25) isn't really a living.

The people opposing the minimum wage increase have several arguments.

These are kids; they don't need much money? They're not; 88% are 20 or older, and the average age of the minimum wage worker is 35.

It's just pocket money; they're not living on it. Well, not very well, anyway. More than half work full time and on the average, they earn half of their family's total income.

If they had more ambition, they could find a higher paying job. Probably not, at least since 2008. However, the depressed job market won't last forever, and when it does improve significantly, the good employees will find higher paying jobs, and the law of adverse selection will kick in with a vengeance. Low-paying corporations will be left with low performing employees.

It's said that Henry Ford didn't really pay his employees twice the going wage so that they could afford his cars; he paid it to avoid the 300% turnover he was experiencing. He was smart enough to know that recruiting and training new employees was a lot more expensive than paying existing employees twice the market rate. That's still true.

There are some things that I learned from being in business for more than 40 years. People tend to do what they're paid to do. If you want really good people, you have to provide a better environment than their other options, and that means (but is not limited to) higher pay. Corporations are not job creators. They are employers. They only hire more people when the business demands it. Customers are job creators.

And there's one thing that I simply believe, having been president, owner, and chief risk taker. No CEO is worth 1250 times as much as any employee.

Perhaps there is some alternate reality where giving more money to the rich makes sense. Unfortunately, that is not the reality we have to live in.

What makes good art?

Aging is a fairly frequent topic here. Those of us who sometimes feel that we're teetering on the brink tend to think about it a lot, even when the AARP mailers don't show up every day. Given the paucity of alternatives to aging, we have to deal with it somehow.

In talking to similarly afflicted friends, I've found that there are a couple of common ways of dealing with aging.

The first, the one I'm most familiar with, is fighting a continued and continually-losing read-guard action, trying to reconcile my mind (who still thinks I'm young) with my body (who knows that I'm not).

Then there are those who simply choose to ignore it, like my friend who spent last year building stone columns for his deck and this year getting over building stone columns for his deck.

However, last week I was exposed to still another—and probably better—way to deal with an inevitable problem. Linda and I were visiting my brother and his wife. Ray raises horses, and Marsha paints and teaches art in Boone, NC. The first night we were there we went to the Second Saturday Art Celebration where Marsha and some of her students had work hanging.

A lot of the work had a surreal quality since Marsha's assignment to her students was to "paint a dream." As an example, she showed them one of her works, "My Dream at 60." It's a figure standing in what appears to be a field of flame. When I first looked at it, I thought I recognized the figure, but since her features aren't clear, I couldn't be sure.

I thought about asking Marsha what it meant, but since she believes that the viewer brings his or her own meaning to art, I knew she'd go all Freud on me and ask me what I thought about that. So I snapped a picture with my phone and thought about it. Here's my analysis, for what it may be worth:

The painting is essentially divided into thirds, with two-thirds of it behind the figure, and one-third including the figure and the blank space in front. The two-thirds is roiled with tongues of flame, not exactly the common view of the "good old days." And there are two other points that seem important to me.

One is the calmness of the figure, facing forward. She looks strong and capable. She's not looking over her shoulder in fear or at the ground in sorrow.

The second is that the painting overruns its borders. It's easy to see that the flames move from the canvas to the frame, and we can imagine that it extends beyond that. It's not so easy to see that the "future" side of the painting also extends up to (and probably beyond) the frame. But it's there.

So what is Marsha's "My Dream at 60" saying? I believe that it is, as I mentioned, a different and better way of dealing with aging, one better than actively (and unsuccessfully) fighting it or attempting to ignore it. Marsha's figure is accepting it and continuing to move on. It is true that there is more behind her than in front of her, and it's also true that what is in front is unknown and unknowable, but that doesn't seem to bother her.

There is, I believe, another truth here: our memories of our past don't include the calm moments. Just as "the good is oft interred with their bones," our calm moments often sink beneath the memories of the turbulent. Maybe, based on the picture, I'll make meditating on why we don't value the calm moments more the second thing on my to-do list.

The first thing will be to try to be more like the figure in the painting: accepting where I am in life and being calm and strong as I move forward.

I will not, however, wear an apron. (That's the part I couldn't figure out.)

Marsha told me one time that good art stimulated a reaction in the viewer. It could be rational, or it could be emotional, but it was the connection between the painting and the person. That's what happened to me with this one.

To Stand or To Sit

I always stand up for the Star Spangled Banner. Unless, of course, I'm in the band playing it, where it's considered bad form for anybody but the director and the percussion section to stand up.

And I have essentially given up on wasting my emotional energies on other people's actions that really don't affect me one way or the other.

That's why I ignored the web uproar about Colin Kaepernick's not standing for the National Anthem. He was expressing his opinion, and I was not required either to agree or disagree with it.

Then I saw a meme that had a picture that was supposed to be of Kaepernick's house and a line that essentially said that he had gotten his; so, what is he griping about.

That bothered me.

Kaepernick never said that he was oppressed. He said that his gesture was for what he sees as wrongdoings against African Americans and other minorities in this country. In other words, he was thinking about somebody other than himself. Evidently, something the generator of the meme didn't understand.

That seems to be declining (or has declined) in this country. We seem to have essentially run out of empathy.

We're also much quicker to grasp at no-cost gestures than to actually do something about the problem.

Which brings us back to Kaepernick taking a knee during the National Anthem. For that, we have outrage, an entire police force threatening not to work football games at the stadium, and people calling him the second most hated man in the NFL. But is he really less patriotic to shun the gesture and call for real action for real problems? Is it less patriotic to think that the nation we call the greatest in the world can actually act like the greatest nation in the world for all of its people?

I'm not particularly fond of The Star Spangled Banner as a song. I don't know many musicians who are. Its meter is clunky. Its rhyme scheme is erratic. And when you get to "the land of the free," everybody except the sopranos and tenors mouths the words until the melody comes back into range. But I do admire the sentiment. When Francis Scott Key wrote the words after the shelling of Fort McHenry during the War of 1812, I can imagine that he was really surprised to see the flag still flying the next morning. The young republic was in danger of extinction. There were people who wanted to become an English colony again. We stood a real chance of losing everything we had won just over 30 years before. So "the rockets' red glare, the bombs bursting in air" were a real threat, and the fact that the flag was still waving the next morning meant something.

Fast forward a couple of hundred years, and we have made a good deal of progress. Legal slavery no longer exists. Women and unpropertied men have the vote. Laws regarding civil rights and voting rights were passed. But, to borrow a metaphor from Kaepernick's trade, that's not the goal line. I'm not sure that it's even midfield.

We still have 45,000,000 people living below the federally defined poverty level, and we argue about whether a CEO making $24,000,000 a year can spare another million or so for taxes.

We still have thousands of families going into bankruptcy because of medical bills.

We still have nearly 20% of our population facing hunger every day. For households with children, the "nutritionally insecurity" rate is over 20%.

We still have neighborhoods that are drained of hope and full of unemployment, resentment, and danger. And the best most of us can do is point fingers and suggest that the people living there should make better choices.

Some people are not capable of empathy. It requires that we get outside of ourselves and into the positions of others. It requires imagination. It requires worrying as much about the condition of others as we do about our own condition.

All of that is tough and uncomfortable. That's probably the reason we go for the easier answer. We're proud of ourselves for flying the flag and standing for the National Anthem and so quickly forgive ourselves for doing nothing about the problems that face so many of our countrymen.

Doing something about them isn't about gestures, standing up or sitting down. It's not about singing or playing the anthem. It's not about posting dismissive memes on Facebook. It's about worrying about somebody other than ourselves.

If you read American history, you know we've never been really good at that. We've always been grasping and greedy—from pushing the Indians off of their land to allowing the very rich push the very poor even further down.

Except...

There were times when the United States were really united, and its people joined in common cause. I lived through one of those: World War II. There were profiteers and crooks, of course, but for the most part, the people all joined in to do what they could for their country, whether—like my father and his brothers—it meant going into service, or—for the rest of us—stomping tin cans, growing Victory Gardens, and learning to live on rationed goods. We not only sympathized with those who lost their family members, we had empathy for people who were worse off than we were, knowing that even though we had little, there were people who had nothing.

The social problems we face now are, in their way, similar to the problems we faced during the war in that they require that we as a nation get involved and deal with them.

I don't care whether Colin Kaepernick stands up or sits down. I do care whether the rest of us, seeing that the benefits of citizenship in this country are distributed so unevenly, just sit there. I imagine Kaepernick will stand up when we do.

The Debasement of Important Words

I was called a rather vile, anatomical name on Facebook the other day by someone who disagreed not only with my political tendencies, but with my indirectly correcting one of the misspellings in his post. (That's one of the side effects of being an English major.)

My first reaction was that I would much rather be called nasty names by someone who didn't know me than by someone who did. All the poster knew about me was that we disagreed. If it had been someone who knew me, I would have probably spent time doing some sort of Woody Allen thing trying to decide whether he was right or not.

My second reaction was that words used to mean something, but that they have succumbed to the same deflation of value that the dollar has. The dollar today, by the way, is worth about 12% of the dollar that I earned when I graduated from college. And being called an SOB or A**hole gets maybe 12% of the reaction it got back then.

We used to take our words seriously. Today, at best, we throw them around with just a remnant of their actual meaning. At worst, they are converted into Newspeak, a la 1984. In the former category, we have words like "patriot," "hero," and—in some circles—"Christian." In the latter category, a good example is the War Department going away in 1947 and becoming the Department of Defense in 1949. Since then we've been in a number of armed conflicts, some more understandable than others. Putting aside those that were arguably justified by treaties, we have defended ourselves in my lifetime by invading Panama, Grenada, and Iraq. Another example Newspeak is the "sound science" movement which was more anti-science than anything else, as well as the name of almost every PAC.

Somewhere along the way we've fallen into the Humpty Dumpty mode of linguistics, which is "When I use a word, it means just what I choose it to mean."

And not often enough is there an Alice to say: "The question is whether you can make words mean so many different things." Consequently, the default answer to Alice's question is "Sure."

Take the word "patriot," for instance. In the dictionary, it means someone who's willing to stand up for their country, who is prepared to defend it against enemies or detractors. In grade school, I learned that Patrick Henry was a patriot, along with a bunch of other guys. They risked what they had to create a nation.

Flash forward 200 years and a self-declared "patriot," is standing in front of a county courthouse with AR-15 protesting the proposed construction of a Mosque. It's hard to understand in a country that prides itself, sometimes correctly, on freedom of religion how someone who is attempting to prevent it can be a patriot.

Those of us who disagreed with the invasion of Iraq were called unpatriotic. Those who wore an American flag on their lapel were called patriotic. It's considered patriotic to scream "love it or leave it," but unpatriotic to call attention to the fact that we are not living up to our ideals. We have at some point redefined patriotism as simple slogans, easy acts, and a bullying posture.

It seems that patriotism has devolved to mean "anybody who doesn't see our country the same way I do."

The definition of "hero" got a lot of ink when Donald Trump decided that John McCain was not a hero. He was captured, and the Donald said that he likes people who weren't captured. Putting aside the inanity of that remark, if all that McCain had done was get captured, he wouldn't be a hero. Heroism has to do with what someone does, not what was done to them. However, McCain refused to take the easy way out when the North Vietnamese discovered that they had captured an admiral's son. He refused to be a propaganda tool for them, and it cost him dearly. That, in my opinion, made him a hero.

Some heroes are easy to pick out. Audie Murphey was a hero. He won 33 awards and medals and was, in my opinion, a much better hero than actor. Other heroes are less obvious and more personal. My dad was a hero to me, especially after I was grown, because then I recognized that he had gotten up every day and worked to support his family and had tried to instill good values in us. He, like McCain, could have probably found an easier way, but he didn't.

On the other side is the female soldier who was wounded in Iraq, rescued by a squad of her fellow soldiers, and returned home to a hero's welcome. Based on the newspaper reports, I couldn't figure out why she was a hero; the soldiers who rescued her might well have been.

Then there's the toughest one of all: Christian. I've never spent a lot of time worrying about whether I was a hero; I can't think of anything I've done that would qualify as heroic. However, I have spent a good deal of time worrying about whether I was really being a Christian.

There are a whole bunch of organizations who call themselves Christian and spew hate, but they haven't been successful in hijacking the word. There's still something strange about someone in a white sheet and hood holding a Bible. Most of the sane world understands that's not Christianity (as we should understand that blowing people up is not Islam).

Within the population that we might consider sane, there are a number of definitions of "Christian," some as circular as "someone who adheres to Christianity." A more actionable definition is that Christian means "a follower of Christ." And if we take that seriously, we find that a lot of what's labeled "Christian" is really something else.

For instance, Christianity that teaches the "Prosperity Gospel" doesn't fit the Christ who didn't have a place to lay his head.

The Christianity that shuts others out, whether they be gay, Muslim, other denominations, or nonbelievers, doesn't fit the Christ who went into mobs to preach. You didn't need your ticket punched by anybody to listen to him. And those who say we should let thousands die because of the possibility that some few might be risk to us are not following the Christ who put His own life at risk so that we might have life.

Based on the accounts in the New Testament, Christians are not exclusive, not defensive, and not worshipping for the money.

I'd like to see all three of these words—patriotism, heroism, and Christian—be restricted to their narrower meaning, to be something we both understand and aspire to.

And, as for the words that started this rambling, I'd like for them to be eliminated from common currency so that when they are used they deliver the emphasis that they used to. There was a time when obscenities and curse words carried force.

The Benefits of Low Expectations

In 2015 news anchor Bryan Williams admitted that the story that he had told about being on a helicopter that was struck by an RPG and small arms fire was not true. He had arrived in another helicopter approximately an hour after the damaged helicopter landed.

Williams apologized, was suspended for six months by NBC, and then exiled to MSNBC.

At about the same time, Bill O'Reilly was caught in a similar situation: he claimed to have reported from the war zone in the Falkland Islands during the brief dustup between Argentina and Great Britain, when evidence, including video, showed that he was doing his reporting some 1,200 miles away from the war zone. O'Reilly claimed that everything he said was true and went on commentating for Fox.

I asked a friend of mine who is a Fox News fan why Fox didn't discipline O'Reilly. To me, it looked like the same level of offense as Williams' helicopter story.

My friend said that the difference was that O'Reilly was an entertainer, not a journalist.

In other words, he's not expected to speak the truth. And since he's not expected to tell the truth, there are no consequences when he doesn't.

I suppose that's the reason some people can get away with a lot and others can get away with nothing. We simply don't expect any better.

I had a personal experience with that years ago when Linda and I invited a friend over for dinner. His wife was out of town, and Linda thought it would be a friendly thing to do. The friend accepted but forgot to show up. We sat there waiting while the lasagna got cold.

Linda was understandably miffed, and we ate leftover lasagna for several days, but she got over it fairly quickly because my friend was locally famous for not being anywhere on time. The word on him was that not only didn't he wear a watch, he didn't carry a calendar.

On the other hand, because I have a near-obsession for punctuality, I'm rarely forgiven for being even a little late.

Sometimes I envied my friend.

Now we're back to another, much more important example of the benefits of low expectations. Throughout the primaries and the general election campaign, Donald Trump has committed gaffe after gaffe, slandering entire groups of people because of their ethnicity, religion, and sex. And he's still standing. He blusters through another string of insults, and his supporters just shrug. The really sad thing about his memorable line about shooting someone in the middle of Fifth Avenue and not losing a vote is that—for a large number of Trump supporters—it's probably true.

There appears to be nothing that he can do that will alienate them. They expect no better.

Having low expectations of the man who forgot to come to dinner or of even a talking head on Fox probably isn't dangerous, although I still think Bryan Williams got a raw deal. But that's not the point. The point is whether we can survive actually considering someone for president for whom we have to keep lowering the bar until it can't be lowered any more.

His latest gaffe is a 10-year-old tape of his relationship with women. He, a married man, was talking about trying to seduce a married woman. She shot him down, which is possibly a credit to her taste. He also talked about groping women and walking right up to them and kissing them. He said they'd let him do that because he was a star.

Of course, the internet went wild with some people condemning what he said and others saying that it was a private conversation, happened 10 years ago, and when men get together they talk like that.

Having been a man for a lot of years and having talked to other men, I can testify that all men don't talk like that. I don't. Almost none of my friends do.

But it isn't nearly so much what he said as what it says about him. It says that he's a privileged rich guy who believes that he can do what he wants to whomever he wants and get away with it because he's a star. Seems that he takes that same attitude into other areas of his life, such as his dealings with vendors, reporters, or beauty queens.

The defense of Donald takes some interesting turns, most of them toward the Clintons' reputation. Their attitude is that Bill did it; so we shouldn't criticize Donald. Even if we were to accept that Bill Clinton is as bad as Donald Trump (which I don't) there would still be an important flaw in that argument: we're not being asked to vote for Bill Clinton, but for Hillary, a woman who has built a substantial body of work both with and apart from her husband.

It's true that Donald, thrice married and an admitted adulterer, thinks that Hillary probably isn't faithful to Bill, although he doesn't pretend to have any evidence to support that. I believe that he simply can't conceive of anybody being faithful and not doing whatever they want. So he assumes that Hillary Clinton is that way.

So here we are, a month before electing a president, and we've lowered the bar to the point that a candidate who creates sentence salads and calls them a speech, whose idea of a debate point is to call his opponent "a loser," and who, according to his public persona, is not anyone that I would allow my daughter to date has a real possibility of being elected president.

We have dangerously lowered our expectations. And we are in danger of electing a leader who barely meets (or fails to meet) even those.

ℰ

The Many and Signal Favors of Almighty God

In my history book in the fourth or fifth grade, there was a painting of a group of Pilgrims and Indians gathered around a table. As I recall the story that accompanied it, the Indians had brought food to the Pilgrims, helped them get through the winter, and together they celebrated the harvest at the first Thanksgiving dinner, which was either in 1621 or 1623.

In appreciation, the Pilgrims took the Indians' land.

I think that this may have been at the root of my deep cynical streak. I couldn't help but wonder if we haven't always celebrated Thanksgiving wrong. George Washington, when he proclaimed the holiday in 1789 declared the it was to be a "as a day of public thanksgiving and prayer to be observed by acknowledging with grateful hearts the many and signal favours of Almighty God." Didn't say a word about turkey.

And that's the way I remember it for these many years. My mother was an excellent cook, and Thanksgiving dinner always had good food. My wife is also an excellent cook and laid out many a wonderful Thanksgiving table.

And since the invention of television and the NFL there was always a football game or two to digest to.

But we've gotten a long way from "a day of public thanksgiving and prayer." Probably a long way from gratefulness, too.

Maybe we should, as I'm trying to do here, take several giant steps away from the current climate and get back to basics. With the Pilgrims, having something to be thankful about was easy. They had made it through another hard winter. Although a lot of them had died, not all of them had. Washington in 1789 was probably both surprised and grateful that the young country had made it that far. They had overcome a war, great dissension regarding exactly what kind of country the USA would be, and a Constitutional Convention that was supposed to patch the Articles of Confederation, but instead wrote a whole new Constitution.

I believe that it's as easy for us to find things to be thankful for, both individually and collectively.

Collectively, we can be grateful that our country has been strong enough to overcome the fact that we sometimes make very poor decisions. We're the oldest country in the world under original management, despite spates of genocide, James Buchanan, Slavery, Millard Fillmore, depressions, recessions, and disagreements that rent the body politic right down the middle. Like Washington, we should be both surprised and thankful that we're still here and still have a future.

I can't speak for other individuals, but I can for myself. I'm grateful that, at a time in my life where I have a lot more past than future, I can take pride in what will follow behind me. My children, my children-in-law, and my grandchildren. If my purpose, like any good camper, was to leave the place a little better than I found it, I think I've succeeded.

I'm thankful for a wife who actually believed the "for richer or poorer, in illness and in health, for better or for worse" vows we made and acted on them. We've managed to do all of those things.

And I'm thankful that I can go to lunch with my conservative friends, argue at a level that causes the waitresses to try to remember the 911 number, then exchange a hug as we leave.

Linda reminded me of the great Norman Rockwell Post cover of the family gathered around the table, a harmonious family about to celebrate yet another Thanksgiving. I've experienced a lot of those Thanksgivings, and they make great memories, even the year we did Cornish Game Hens instead of turkey. But, at least for a little while, I think we should go back to Washington's original purpose: "a day of public thanksgiving and prayer to be observed by acknowledging with grateful hearts the many and signal favors of Almighty God."

Happy Thanksgiving.

&

About Walking a Mile in Another's Shoes

All my life I've been told that I shouldn't criticize anyone until I'd walked a mile in their shoes.

In my young and more literal days, I thought that would probably hurt since I had, as my father said, been blessed with a very solid foundation. I envisioned pinched toes, blisters, and all sorts of other foot pains.

After I became older and less literal, I saw that the point wasn't that we should try to put ourselves in the places of others, but that since we cannot walk a "mile in their shoes," we should simply accept that others have different perspectives based on their life experiences.

But today, there seem to be a lot of people attempting to overlay their perspectives on entire groups of people. There are the people who say that poor people are poor just because of the choices they made. That homeless people need to get a job and a home. That people of other religions need to assimilate. That people from other countries need to speak English. In other words, there are a lot of people just like one of my relatives, who contended that (fill in your targeted group here) were fine so long as they knew their place. Then she would describe what that place was.

As a Christian, white male, I have never had to deal with anti-Semitism. I have never had to crawl across a racial barrier or try to crack the glass ceiling. From the distance, I looked just like almost all the CEOs, major league sports figures, and other really rich people. That meant that as a young Public Health Service employee, I could take Linda to dinner at a Country Club (by invitation of a member) that was 100% white and Christian.

The number of barriers I didn't have to deal with were legion. That taught me two things: that whatever success I had was, in a large part, handed to me. I worked hard, hopefully with some skill. But those who didn't have the advantages that I was born with, despite working harder and having more skill, had much more difficulty getting to where I've ended up or even close to it.

As I thought about other peoples' shoes, three examples popped into my mind, two of which I hadn't thought of in years.

The first was a house I visited as an investigator when I was with the public health service. (Turned out that when I graduated from college, VD investigators were not only in more demand than writers, but were better paid.) There was a grandmother in her late 30s, her daughter, and her daughter's daughter. When I went up on the porch I noticed that front door was missing. So was the screen door. All that was left was the frame, and the flies flew in and out unimpeded.

The people who lived there didn't have a long horizon line; they essentially lived from day to day with some days being better than others. They didn't have a budget because they had no money. They didn't have a career plan because—with no education—there was no career. And I imagine that they didn't have hope because they had no real concept of hope.

But we have the self-righteous among us who claim that these people are in their situation because of their poor choices. But I wonder if they ever had any real choices at all.

The second example is a homeless person that I met when I volunteered in a shelter. I've written about him before because he made such an impression on me. Joe had once had a real life, one where he made decisions and had choices, but his mental illness had separated him from decisions and choices and left him on the street, afraid of everything around him. The shelter at Clifton Presbyterian took care of him as well as they could, within the bounds of rules, insurance liability, and financial resources. But Joe was still on the street every day, dragging his fears with him and enduring the hard looks of the people who were sure he could do better. But when your greatest hope is that the food they served you at the shelter isn't poisoned, there's not much better he could do.

And, finally, there was Sonya's mother. Sonya was a beautiful Polish woman who married an American soldier shortly after World War II and returned to the United States with him. She worked for years to bring her parents from Communist-ruled Poland to this country. When I met her parents, I noticed that her mother's face was slightly misshapened; Sonya explained that a soldier had knocked out her teeth and broken her jaw with a rifle butt. The father took to American life, but the mother just sat there. She couldn't understand the ways. She couldn't speak the language. The fact that she was fluent in both Polish and German didn't help much in a small North Carolina town. Finally, she decided to go back to Poland; a repressive government in a country with people she knew was better for her last days than a Democracy where she was isolated. She and her husband went back, and a lot of people were surprised.

163

The point is that, even if I could walk a mile in the shoes of any of these, it wouldn't inform my understanding of them. For any of them, it wasn't just a mile, but many miles, and some of them very hard. I have no right to say that the black women in Macon should buy a door, get a job, and live like me. I have no right to look at Joe and say get off the street, cut your tangled beard, and be a productive member of society. And I have no right to tell Sonya's mother that all she needs to do is assimilate; this is a great place and you'll love it.

Because I don't have the slightest idea what brought them to the point I encountered them.

I do have the right to help them however I can. I do have the right to work to remove the barriers that will create more like them. And—at the very least—I have the right to treat them as individuals whose experiences I cannot imagine. Which should keep me from feeling self-righteous and superior.

Just keep in mind what Jesus said on the subject: "If you love only those who love you, why should you get credit for that? Even sinners love those who love them!

Have yourself a Merry.

It's amazing what you can learn by reading the funeral industry's trade publications. For instance, I learned that in the two weeks around Christmas and New Year's, there a spike of between 3% and 9% in terms of natural deaths. There is not, contrary to the persistent myth, a spike in suicides.

I think that the reason the Christmas suicide myth has hung around so long is that a lot of us don't subscribe to the "merry," "jolly," or "happy" descriptions of the holidays, leaning more toward the "blue," "depressive," and "dejected" side.

There are probably a lot of reasons for this. Some of us just don't have the personality to get up to "merry" and sustain it. I've contended for years that I have about a 24-hour Merry Christmas window. Some of us had disappointing Christmases as children, and probably more of us have had disappointing Christmases as adults. When we're kids, we're disappointed that we didn't get something we wanted. When we're adults, we're disappointed that haven't given those we love something that they want.

In my children's generation, it was about giving them what we didn't have, which resulted in staying up all night putting toys together and hoping that they would last through Christmas day. To this day, I haven't forgiven the designers of the Lost in Space game or of Barbie's Townhouse.

Now, with the grandchildren, I don't know what the stories will be. Perhaps that Santa couldn't fit the Prius into his sleigh. That'll be for generations to come.

But I do know this: Christmas doesn't do this to us. We do it to ourselves by getting caught up in something that has little or nothing to do with Christmas. That's how roughly 25% of the annual retail spending is done during the Christmas season. And along with each of these purchases comes a hundred unanswered questions and a load of guilt because we don't always have the answers. "Is this what she really wants?" "Is it the right size (color, cut, etc.)." Have I treated all of the equivalent relations equivalently?" "What does 'usually shipped in two to six days' really mean when it's eight days until Christmas?"

One way out of this would be to give everybody an orange, then contribute the balance of the $752 (2016's average expenditure on Christmas gifts) to a homeless shelter or a similar cause in keeping with the spirit of Christmas.

But most of us are not going to do that. I'm sure that my basic Christmas guilt at not doing what I should for all of those I love would be exponentially expanded. Instead, to get through the season without pouting or spreading gloom to all around me, I've adopted three basic tactics:

1. I'll actually put thought into selecting the gifts I give; so, I can actually tell myself I tried. If I fail, I fail. Won't be the first time.

2. I'll try to take every opportunity to pass along a feeling of good cheer to everyone I encounter, even the guy who ran the stop sign and almost took off the front of my car. I smiled and waved to him with all five fingers.

3. I won't pass up an opportunity to give to those I don't know. In the multiple levels of charity described by the Jews, the greatest is where neither the giver nor receiver is known to the other. That works for Christmas, too.

Beyond that, we'll do what we do every Christmas: try to keep some focus on what we as Christians are really celebrating. It has nothing to do with trees, gifts, ornaments, or parties. It has everything to do with the birth of the Christ child, a gift that cannot disappoint us.

Cowardly Christians

Twice this week I have been warned of an impending takeover of the United States by Muslims and once I have been asked to vote on whether Sharia Law should be banned in the United States.

I am offended, deeply offended. However, it's not because we're going to be taken over by the Muslims. I don't believe that.

The only Muslim friend I've ever had played trumpet in a band that I was in years ago. We'd take our breaks out back, smoke, and discuss religion. His father was one of the founders of a mosque in a Midwestern city. As best I could tell, he practiced his religion faithfully, blew his trumpet slightly better than I played reeds, and worried about the same things I did. Not once did he mention taking over the United States.

Besides, Muslims comprise only 1% of our population. More likely, native Americans would come back to get what we took away from them, and they make up 2% of the population.

That should also take care of the fear of Sharia Law. 1% probably won't impose its will on the other 99%. And if the 1% wants to observe the parts of Sharia that don't contravene US laws, that shouldn't be a problem either. We've had Hasidic Jews strictly following the 613 laws found in the Torah for centuries, and they've never tried to take over the United States. They have lived apart, but at peace with their neighbors. And I've never seen memes warning me that they were coming for my barbecue and shellfish.

The absolute lack of logic in the rabble-rousing memes and the silliness of thinking we're going to begin cutting off the hands of thieves under Sharia Law isn't what offends me. That level of thinking is becoming so common as to be unremarkable these days.

What does offend me is that people who purport to be Christian feel that our faith is so weak that we can be blown over by any wind that passes by. Not just Muslims, but by a department store clerk saying, "Happy Holidays." That our marriages are jeopardized by the rights of homosexuals to be married and our faith weakened by the law that says our churches can't tell congregations how to vote.

According to these people, to survive, we must encode our religious beliefs into the law.

All of this, however, fails to recognize Christianity is at its strongest when it does not have the state at its back, but when it's forced to rely on the strength of God to do God's work.

Otherwise, we tend to deal in empty gestures.

In 1954, Congress decided we needed to do something to separate ourselves from "godless Communism." It sounded like a good idea, but instead of expecting our Christians to act more Christian, their solution was to add the words "under God" to the Pledge of Allegiance.

Or, in Georgia, the legislature took up the "Pastor Protection Act," aiming to protect pastors from the invading hordes of homosexuals seeking weddings. I have yet to talk to a pastor who thought he or she needed protection.

Or several of our current politicians declaring that we must institutionalize Christian values in our schools and other public places, putting prayer in schools and the 10 Commandments on the courthouse lawn.

Forget that most of these things wouldn't pass Constitutional muster. Think about what it says about our faith.

Do this: walk into a church with stained glass windows. Try to find one depicting the judge who insisted on a stone monument to the 10 Commandments or the legislator who took the well to propose that have a law that protects our pastors. There will, I hope, never be a Christian memorial to an empty gesture.

On the other hand, consider what brought Christianity from a small group of people in an insignificant Roman province to a force throughout the world. Those are the things that we memorialize.

St. Stephen choosing to kneel and pray for his attackers as the stones pounded him. Saul watched.

Saul, now Paul, sometimes sick and weak, going from one city to another preaching the Gospel, and sometimes narrowly escaping with his life.

The Christians who faced the law and might of Rome and gave up their lives in testimony to their Faith.

Roger Williams tramping alone through the snow to leave the institutionalized church and found a denomination separate from the government.

The Christians who risked their lives ferrying slaves to freedom.

The Christians who risked their lives saving Jewish children from the Nazis in the last century.

The Christians who put themselves between authority and those oppressed by that authority.

Their weapon was unselfish, unflinching love.

No, I don't believe that Islam is going to overcome Christianity and that we will all be subjected to Sharia law. But I do think that it's a distinct possibility that Christianity will fall of its own lack of faith, in its all-consuming interest in dictating the acts of others, and under the weight of empty gestures used to replace self-sacrifice.

On June 19, 1945, Dietrich Bonhoeffer was executed because of his activity against the Reich. Bonhoeffer's motive was that he could not abide the way Hitler's government was treating the Jews. First, he opposed it. Then he attempted to take direct action. To me, the important point is that this Christian did not ignore the treatment of non-Christians. He fought it, even unto death.

There is probably no cure for those who think that Sharia law is going to become the law of the land. Or that we can be Christian and deny help to those being killed, no matter what faith or race they are. Or that we can substitute a gesture for an action.

However, there are the rest of us, those who cling to the spirit of a 2000-year history of showing extravagant love without counting the cost.

Keep in mind that Jesus did not go to the Sanhedrin and ask for a law. He went to the streets and then to the Cross.

Fear doth make cowards of us all.

Last night I think I got a glimpse of why so many people are so worried about immigrants.

On Jeopardy!

It was the final night of the Jeopardy College Championship, and the three contestants were a Stanford student of Indian descent, a Naval Academy freshman whose last name was Tshu, and an MIT student from Decatur, Georgia of Chinese descent. Not a one up there looked like me, even when I was their age.

Then it occurred to me that those people who are ranting about immigrants may well be scared. They're having to compete against immigrants who are smarter, willing to work harder, and sacrifice more. So, instead of stepping up their game to compete with them, they ask the government to shut them out. They don't seem to realize that every time they have a rally saying that they are coming to take our jobs, what they are really saying is that we don't think we can compete with them.

They're scared.

And they may have good reason to be scared. More than half the patents issued in the United States are issued to people who were not born here. And three-quarters of the patents issued to the top ten patent-producing universities had at least one foreign-born inventor. The natives of the country that has for years held itself to be the leader in innovation have essentially left the field.

And it's not just the nerds. The immigrants make a big impact on what we (sometimes erroneously) call unskilled jobs. We proved it in Georgia.

In 2011, State Representative Matt Ramsey and his like-minded colleagues wrote a bill entitled HB87. According to Forbes, he said that the goal "was to eliminate incentives for illegal aliens to cross into our state." That may have been the goal, but the result was that South Georgia farmers suffered an estimated $140,000,000 in agricultural losses as crops rotted in the field.

The idea was that if the immigrants didn't take the jobs away, locals would be employed. Most of them didn't last a day. They didn't have either the drive, the strength, or the skills to effectively harvest the crops. Then Georgia decided that they would dispatch prisoners to harvest the crops. That didn't work either.

This is what happens when you do things like Matt Ramsey and his buddies did. Or like the current President and his buddies are doing. They approach the subject of immigration reform like a horticulturist pruning a rosebush with a hatchet. And like that, the results aren't pretty.

Anyone who knows me might say that because I'm old and no longer really competing I can afford to have such a sanguine attitude to the (insert color or ethnicity here) horde. And that's true. But both my children and their spouses go to work every day in places where multiple languages are spoken and many of their coworkers aren't from around here.

In fact, when my son married his bride, it was a sort of segregated reception, segregated by dietary restrictions. We had Chinese food at several tables and at least one table of Indian food. My wife and I sat at the international table and ate Chinese food. It was delicious.

To me, my children and children-in-law have the right idea. They get up in the morning, go to work, and do the level of work that it takes to succeed in that environment.

I don't know anyone who thinks that we shouldn't have immigration laws. Obviously, we should, but we need to have sane ones, levels of immigration that not only serve the needs of our country, but provide a path to success for those who come into this country from other places.

In my lifetime you could pretty well map the immigration process from the names on the major league baseball teams. By the time I began paying attention, the dominance of the Irish players (O'Rourke, Casey, McGraw, Doyle, Kelly, etc.) and the Jewish players (Cohen, Berg , Arnovich, Feldman, etc.) had given way to the Italians (the Dimaggios, Rizutto, Berra, Campanella, etc.), then to what we called Negro baseball players, beginning with Jackie Robinson and soon becoming numerous, on up to Spanish speaking players. New groups came in, competed, and they did take away some jobs, but because they did them better.

That's the way it's always been, and I really doubt that there anyway we can stop it now. Nor should we.

There are three things I think we should do, and since I know very little about immigration, I offer these as possible suggestions with details to be worked out (if ever) by people who do know something.

First we should recognize the difference between immigration reform and xenophobia. Right now our politicians are using immigration as a blunt instrument to keep the base stirred up.

Secondly, we should make sure that immigrants we do let in are treated properly. Our country has a sorry history of immigrant labor. Read about the Chinese who came here to build our railroads, or the middle Europeans who worked in Chicago's slaughter houses, or the Jews who did piecework in New York. And that, of course, is not mentioning the most flagrant human violation of all: the Africans who involuntarily immigrated to support the plantation economy. It's surprising that generations of the Chinese, Japanese, Poles, Czechs, Jews and dozens of other immigrant nationalities haven't risen up against us. Instead, in a large part, they managed to work their way up, and some became very successful.

Finally, we should create an immigration program that is no longer shrill and political, but is sane and businesslike. We can start with the fact that to maintain any position of leadership in the world, we need the immigrants, those with Ph.D.s and those who know how to harvest vegetables. Then we can determine how we can balance this against the security concerns we have without looking callous and dumb to the rest of the world.

I don't know how to do it, but I know that there are a lot of people out there smarter and better informed than I am. I hope—in the words of that great philosopher Larry, the Cable Guy— they'll get'er done.

Staring into the Abyss

They are things we've been doing for years. Not being able to come up with the name of the guy who starred in the movie. Standing in front of the open refrigerator wondering why we opened it. Putting our car keys down somewhere, but nobody knows where.

We've been doing them for years, but there's a difference.

When we were younger, we just chalked it up to being distracted, inattentive, or careless. Now that we are older we wonder if this is the beginning of something awful.

Age does that to you. What used to be disconnected events become symptoms.

We all know someone or know a family member of someone who has Alzheimer's or some other dementia. We see the toll it takes on the family as they watch somebody they love drift further and further away. We wonder if the lost car keys might be the beginning of that.

We know that nearly 14% of people our age are diagnosed with Alzheimer's or vascular dementia, people who are alive, but not living. And that becomes our greatest fear: outliving our lives and simply being a dead weight on those who love us.

When you get old and have assorted aches and pains, it's hard to be consistently optimistic. It's hard to take a rational view. That view would be if nearly 14% have some sort of dementia, more than 86% of us don't. We are not destined to go out like a flickering light bulb.

I have good role models to fall back on. My mother's father and my father's mother each died at 75. Granddaddy did it just like he wanted to. He frequently said that he wanted to die at the wheel of a new car. After he closed his service station, he went to work for the Pontiac dealer and got a brand new demonstrator. One morning he got in the car, backed out of the driveway, pulled to the curb across the street and died. Just as he had wanted to: at the wheel of a new car.

Grandmother wasn't quite so fortunate. She had a stroke and didn't recover consciousness for six months. But until the day of the stroke, she was active, outspoken, and—without question—the matriarch of the clan.

I only visited her a couple of times while she was in the nursing home, and it didn't matter either time. But, sitting there, I discovered it was a lot more fruitful to think about the many years that she was active and very much alive than to concentrate on the shrinking husk in the bed.

That's a lesson that kept coming back to me this week. I console myself that I haven't lost a step, simply because I've never had a step. My mind is still reasonably active. And I don't yet drool in public. Getting old is not fun, but it's not nearly as dreadful as we sometimes make it.

I'm writing this as a pep talk to myself. I've lost a pen that Linda gave me. We've looked everywhere, and it's nowhere. Some of my moving parts don't really want to move. And I find myself thinking that in front of every silver lining there's a cloud.

But, those are just incidents and attitudes. They are not symptoms.

At our age, we do spend time staring into the abyss. But nothing says we have to jump in.

Racial Attitudes in the Post-Acceptance Era

Last week I had two insights about race in the world around me. I doubt either of them is particularly original, but it was enough to make me think.

The first was during a lunch with an old friend. I've known him for fifty years, and I know he's not a racist. I've observed him liking, disliking, admiring, and loathing people without regard to race, creed, color, or sexual identity. I've also seen him go out of his way to help a number of people who were not of his racial persuasion.

In the fifty years we've been talking, debating, and arguing, he's moved further and further to the right, and sometimes our luncheon conversations scare the waitresses and cause people in nearby booths to sink down in their seats. But the fact that we disagree doesn't keep us from being friends and enjoying our occasional lunches.

At this one, in the middle of our discussion of the Republican budget bill, he looked at me and said:

"One of these days you'll realize that all those old boys back where we came from were right. They are different from us."

My immediate response was "So what?", but later I realized that there was a lesson in that.

The lesson was that even if we're not racists, we think racially. That means that I will might respond differently to a someone of a different race than someone of my own, even under exactly the same conditions. It's the old story about people crossing the street to avoid large black men, but it's carried out in a hundred subtle ways. It's reflexive, the product of our conditioning.

It would be comforting to say that our racial conditioning informs our responses. But it would be wrong. "Inform" implies that it helps us make more accurate assessments and react more properly. But that's not the case; it influences our assessments and reactions. And I can't imagine that all of the subtle differences in our actions go unnoticed by those on the other end of them.

The line between being racist and thinking racially is indistinct, and it's probably set by the person who experiences our action.

The day after my lunch with my friend I attended my grand-daughter's fifth-grade graduation. She goes to an extremely diverse elementary school; it's like a Tower of Babel with a large English-as-a-Second-Language class. The program was full of names like Aguilar, Ashihel, Aybar, Xia, Jovanovic, Kabir, Machacuay, Zhang, and Soun, along with names such as Harper, Harrington, Benfield, and Brown.

The school does well in statewide competitions, with teams reaching the state in reading, science, and other "bowls."

Their science fair projects go well beyond building the traditional papier-mâché volcano. When they presented the certificates to the science fair winners, I could admire their efforts, but I had no idea what most of them had done. One of them had to with green beans.

It is, by almost any standard, a successful school. And in the cafetorium that morning there was a lot of enthusiasm, a good bit of nostalgia, and constant reminders that these students were entering a new stage in their life and education.

In her opening remarks, the principal said that the kids had brainstormed the attributes that they thought they should be remembered for, and when she read the list, you could tell that they were pleased with what they were (or wanted to be). The list included the following: smart, funny, joyous, energetic, happy and four or five other equally positive qualities. I noticed that they didn't include "accepting." I thought that, given that there were a so many kids that "were different from us," acceptance would be a large and positive thing.

But as I watched them march across the stage, get their certificates and awards, and hug the principal, I had my second insight: these kids didn't need to add "acceptance" to their list of positives. They were beyond that.

To say that you "accept" something or someone implies the power to reject that same thing. There is still an imbalance of power. In the world in which my granddaughter lives, the difference in race and ethnic origin is simply a matter of fact, on a par with hair color and right or left handedness.

These are kids who can not only pronounce a name like Xia or Zacahua-Varela with no problem, but will shout it loudly when that student's picture comes up on the screen. They probably wouldn't understand all of the things that were going through my mind as I watched them get their awards.

And, for that, I am truly thankful.

When I was a small child, I was taught that "red and yellow, black and white, they are precious in His sight." With luck, these children may get to actually live that.

Unless, of course, we older people change their minds.

The Party of Pangloss

The recent election of Donald J. Trump to the presidency of the United States has spurred a renewed interest in literature. Novels such as *Brave New World*, *1984*, and *It Can't Happen Here* are frequently discussed and probably occasionally read. They all seemed to portend things to come.

I didn't take Trump seriously for a long time. And I was obviously wrong. I underestimated the credulity of people who would accept things they wanted to hear, even in the face of reality to the contrary.

That made me think of another book that seemed to be relevant to our times, even though it was written in another country about 250 years ago. I can imagine Voltaire sitting at his desk with his quill in one hand and scratching his head with the other, wondering why there were people out there whose minds seemed to believe what their eyes and ears should have belied. They had lived through the Seven Years War, the Lisbon earthquake, and a lot of other things that weren't as much fun as they should have been; yet they believed with an optimistic fervor.

There are any number of things in this old book that recommend it for our current society. For instance, there is wealth inequality. Candide, illegitimate son of a Baron, manages about a new adventure per page and eventually finds himself in South America, in a country run by priests, known collectively as Los

Padres. It doesn't take long for him to understand the economic structure of the company.

Los Padres owned everything, and the poor owned everything else.

And there's Candide's look at religion and charity. At this point the poor soul is down on his luck, having been kicked out of the palace for kissing the Baron's daughter. He wanders, penniless, until he comes to a preacher preaching charity. He humbly begs for some money for food, and the preacher asks him a theological question. When Candide doesn't answer in accord with the preacher's beliefs, the preacher chases him off.

And there's the peculiar logic propounded by the characters. "The nose was formed so that we might have spectacles. Our legs were formed so that we might have trousers." It is a world of cause and effect, but it's questionable as to which was which.

But none of those things made me think of Candide, a book I hadn't read in some sixty years. What did make me think of it was a brief post on Facebook that said, "Donald Trump is the best president this country's ever had." I thought, "My goodness, Pangloss lives!"

Pangloss is, to me, the most interesting character in *Candide*, even though he's absent from the entire middle of the book. We leave him early on, when he is being hanged because it's raining too hard to burn him, and we meet him again near the end of the book where he is a galley slave (and not a very good one).

The thing about Pangloss is that he is so blinded by his ideology that he must conform his beliefs to that no matter what violence he must do to reality to make it fit. An example:

Pangloss is explaining to Candide how Pangloss had become infected with syphilis. He recites the sequence of infection all the back to a crewmember on one of Columbus' boats, but says that he'll pass it to no one, because he is dying of it. Candide makes sympathetic noises, but is assured by Pangloss that this is way that it should be. "It (symphilis) is an indispensable feature of the best of all possible worlds, a necessary ingredient: for if Columbus, in an island off the Americas, had not contracted this disease—which poisons the source of all procreation, and often even prevents procreation, contrary though this be to nature's greatest plan—we would have neither chocolate nor cochineal."

Pangloss is, however, cured by an Anabaptist, and the cure only costs him an eye and an arm.

Pangloss, even after the syphilis, being hanged, being dissected by the barber who thought he was dead, and being sold into slavery, hung on to his ideology, that this is the best of all possible worlds. You get the feeling that he had to; if he let that go, he would have been left with nothing. It's not until the last few pages of the book that Voltaire reveals his solution to all of this. Candide; the Baron; the once-beautiful, now-ugly Cunegonde; and Paquette, the housemaid who gave syphilis to Pangloss, finally abandoned their ideology and retired to a farm to cultivate their garden. And they prospered.

Although the latter-day Panglosses seem to have a different philosophy—Save us, save us, we're all going to die—they tend to hold on to it in the face of overwhelming evidence to the contrary.

It is true that we're all going to die, but not of the things that Donald Trump is peddling.

One of the sadder things we have to face is that when *Candide* was written, it was intentionally broad satire. Now, it's pretty much our political reality.

&

Ghost Stories

I have discovered that when you've grown old your mind wanders down dark roads kicking up dusty recollections and strange memories. That happened to me this week after I heard about the six teenagers killed in two separate accidents.

Two of them—brothers—were on their way to a dentist appointment. Four were going somewhere else; the news didn't say. Because of the accidents, there were six young people who in one moment had futures and in the next didn't.

And we'll never know what possibilities were cut off in that instant between having a future and not having one.

For some reason, that made me think of two people from my distant past.

One—J.R. Register—was a classmate. J.R. played trumpet in the band and was on the basketball team. I don't remember what J.R. planned to do with his life; I'm sure he had the same kind of aspirations and plans the rest of us had. At least until a driver ran a stop sign on a country road one night and killed both J.R. and his date.

The other one was Joanne Neighbors. Joanne was older than we were, the older sister of Keith who, among other things, was the trumpet player in our wanna-be Dixieland band. Joanne had graduated from Meredith with a degree in music and was blessed with perfect pitch. She patiently sat through Sunday afternoon practices in their living room, occasionally writing out a part to fill in a hole an arrangement.

The week before Christmas that year Joanne was in Four Oaks to conduct a church's Christmas cantata. They found her in her car.

Unlike J.R., Joanne already had her path set. She had won awards for her compositions and was being recognized for unusual talent. She had a cousin who was a nationally known composer, and it looked as if Joanne was going to do just as well. Until that night.

My mental wanderings are not as morbid as they sound. This is not some sort of survivor's guilt. What I was thinking about was unrealized possibilities and what that should mean for those of us who still have a future. Sometimes I think we are so busy with the here-and-now that we don't invest in our futures; we don't keep working toward those possibilities. And I don't think old age is a good excuse for that. It's true that we've arrived at a point where we obviously have more past than future, but that isn't license to give up on the future we do have.

In short, I believe that just the act of waking up in the morning places a responsibility on us to lead meaningful lives, to accept the gift of another day gratefully and to use it purposefully.

There is, when you get older, a tendency to mentally cut life off, to decide that something would be a good idea, but there's probably not enough time for that. You decide not to try to learn another skill or another language, to begin a large project, or to dive into some activist group. Unconsciously, we are just picking a place to die.

But look at the other side: if you decide to launch into a major project and you don't have an opportunity to finish it, what have you lost? Even unfinished, the project has added purpose to the days you did have.

Back in the forties, cowboys kept saying they wanted to die with their boots on. I didn't really have any idea what that meant until I got older. It meant that, if they were going to be cut down, they wanted it to be when they were active rather than lingering in bed. Now I can understand that, but I still feel that it's incomplete. To me, it's not so much that we have our boots on, but that even our last and final steps are going somewhere. We still have purpose.

We'll never know what J.R. and Joanne would have accomplished if they had lived to an old age; it's not really helpful to speculate on it. But there's always our own future, long or short, that we're responsible for. And may we really make the most of it.

Once Upon a Time in America

It was a damp, hot Saturday in Mobile in 1962, and I was a young Public Health Service employee who probably wasn't much use to anyone. But it was an important day, and I remember three things about it.

It was a very long day. From the time we opened the doors that morning, people walked through the gymnasium, getting their sugar cubes. They weren't noisy; they just shuffled along in their place in line. Since I was standing in one place, it was just one face replacing another.

A very large lady brought a very large pot of gumbo and some plastic bowls and spoons over just after noon. With all the planning that had gone into that day, no one had thought about how, in a fifteen-hour day, we were going to eat. It was—and is—the only gumbo I've had that didn't come from a restaurant kitchen or a can, and it is still the best I've ever eaten.

For once in my life, I was part of something much bigger than myself. This was happening all over the state of Alabama and throughout the country. We were going to eradicate polio.

I knew something about polio. In 1948, the disease hit my home town with a vengeance. The four-year-old who lived on the street behind us contracted it and died. One of the daughters of the family three doors up the street from us was wheeled out on a stretcher, put in an ambulance, and taken to the hospital. She limped for the rest of her life. Polio was like an attacking army, leaving dead and wounded in its wake. The swimming pool and the movie theatre were closed; it wasn't a good idea to get crowds of people together.

I was shipped off to Blacksburg, Virginia. When the parents there learned I was from North Carolina, they kept their children away from me.

The Salk vaccine, introduced in 1955 had made a big dent in the incidence of polio, and the Sabin vaccine, more effective and delivered orally, was supposed to deliver the knock-out blow. It worked. The incidence of polio in the United States dropped from 3190 in 1960 to 122 in 1964. It continued to drop, and there's only been one confirmed case of polio in the US in the 21st century.

The reason for all this remembering is not to take a leisurely stroll down memory lane but to try to answer a question I've been pondering for the past week. The question is how do thoughtful people stare at the same facts and come up with radically different opinions. It's worse than the three blind men and the elephant.

I have a number of conservative friends. They are not greedy, grasping people. They don't have horns and tails. and I'm sure that they don't really want anyone to die from lack of health care or food. We engage in prolonged and sometimes complex discussions. They bring facts to their arguments. I try to do the same thing. Yet we disagree on a fundamental question: What is the role of government in solving society's challenges.

None of my friends are as blunt (or as wrong) as the man quoted in the paper this morning who said, "If the government is behind it, it's going to fail." About the strongest statement in one of our discussions was that "the government is rarely the solution."

Then why do some of feel that more government involvement is the solution and others believe that less—or no government—involvement is the solution.

The answer I finally came up with is that I have seen and occasionally been a part of government programs that worked and made our country a better place. While I believe that America's greatness at any point may well be a matter of where you were standing at that time, I know from my own experience that there have been occasions of greatness when the American government and the American people made history.

I lived through a war where we went from a minor military power with fewer than a half-million citizens under arms to the defender of democracy and winner with more than 12 million under arms. I saw what we did to help salvage the European economy after the war and to supply Berlin during the blockade. After the war, the soldiers came back and went to school and bought homes under the GI Bill. More than 5,000,000 used it to continue their education. They became our teachers, executives, and professionals. The fact that the number of college graduates doubled from before the war to after the war changed our society.

We initiated a space program that put a man on the moon and is still exploring the far reaches of our universe.

Social security, a product of Roosevelt's New Deal, still provides a bit of security for our oldest and weakest, and Medicare—a part of Johnson's Fair Deal—works better for me than any private health plan that I've had. (And I'm essentially a stress test for any health plan.)

Dwight Eisenhower signed the law to create the Interstate Highway system in 1956 and now we have nearly 50,000 miles of Interstates crossing the nation, and it's probable that most of our citizens have been on one or more them this week.

Because of the government, we've managed to abolish official racial and gender discrimination. At least in the eyes of the federal government, all men and women are created equal.

There's something that all of these successful government programs have in common: not one of them is defensive. They were created to accomplish something rather than to keep others from accomplishing something. (Nit-pickers may want to say that our involvement in WWII was defensive, but what I remember is that we were out to save the world from the Fascists.)

I believe that it isn't that government programs don't work, but that it's that we have allowed a government that serves masters rather than citizens, that we're more interested in what we can keep others from doing than in what great things we can do, and that the stirring words of Roosevelt, Kennedy, and Johnson have become piteous whines and moans about those who are out to get us. It isn't that government cannot be the answer so much as it's the government as we've defined it has no answers.

To misquote Shakespeare, "the fault, dear Conservative, is not in our government, but in ourselves." So long as we allow ourselves to be led about by people who have nothing to offer us but shelter from fears, it may well be true that the government is rarely the solution. But my experience is that big, ambitious, and sometimes controversial government programs can work—if you define "work" as creating a better, smarter, and stronger country with opportunities for its citizens.

In other words, I believe that our government can, as nearly every other advanced country has done, make certain that all citizens have good health care. It can also provide greater access to all levels of education, from pre-school through secondary to post-secondary, whether that be vocational or college.

Credit Where Credit is Due

A couple of years ago my brother, yet another ink-stained wretch who makes his living stringing words together, asked me if I knew how one family from Benson produced two writers who could survive (and occasionally thrive) by writing.

It's not that Benson didn't have its share of successful people. Some were nationally known: a composer who taught, composed and lived out his life at the Cincinnati Conservatory; the very influential CEO of a major bank; one of the county's best guitar players and a fixture at the Grand Ol' Opry, among others. Then there are any number who were successful, but not known outside the confines of Benson.

But—of writers, there was a dearth.

I did know and still do. She would have been 96 tomorrow.

My brothers and I learned valuable lessons from each of our parents. They both modeled the kind of behavior that caring, civilized, and sometimes courageous people exhibited. And they both cared for their children. In fact, I've often attributed my lack of success in fiction writing to the fact that I couldn't complain about my childhood. My brothers and I had loving parents who gave us everything they could afford and then some.,

However, the influence in the particular sphere of words had to come from mother. Dad was a man of few words and much preferred things he could add up.

There were two things that mother gave us that I believe pushed Pat and me into writing. The first was environmental, and the second was, for lack of a better word, philosophical.

The environmental element was mother's love of books. She had a lot of books, and they covered a wide variety of subjects. She probably owned the only set of Will Durant's *Story of Civilization* in Benson. It's 11 volumes and about as dense as lead. They're on my bookshelves now, and I've read some of them.

Mother belonged to the Book of the Month club for years, and I can only imagine what she had to give up to keep up with the BOM charges, but I do know she considered it worthwhile. She spent a lot of time in her recliner reading.

That, through either genetics or osmosis, became an important part of our lives. Mother read. We read. And we could sit in the same room for long periods of time, just reading and not talking.

They say that one of the basics of good writing is good reading. We got that from mother.

But there was an even more important influence, I think. Mother was certainly a product of her time and place; yet she didn't let that confine her. She, like so many others in the rural South (and probably the rural North) dropped out of school at an early age. She also married at an early age. And became a mother at an early age. For so many that was a trap, both economically and socially. But not for her.

She became the living embodiment of the Browning line: "Ah, but a man's reach should exceed his grasp, Or what's a heaven for?"

It wasn't so much what she reached for for herself as what she wanted for her children. Early on, it was assumed that we would be reared to proper gentlemen (in a day when that defined a standard of behavior). And we were, although it was sometimes either painful or embarrassing or both. Later, it was assumed that we would do well in school, an assumption that was met with mixed results, but still more uniform than dad's assumption that we would, like him, excel at sports.

Finally, it was assumed that we would go to college. This was at a time when more than a third of students left high school before graduation—and that's a national statistic. It may well have been higher in Johnston County, where so many students left school to work on the family farm. And that was a time when fewer than a third of college-age people went to college.

The question that was never really addressed so far as I can remember was: how are you going to send three boys to college when you can't afford it?

I'm not sure mother ever thought in those terms.

Nor did it really seem to concern her that all three of us majored in studies that didn't make us more occupationally desirable. Dad wanted us to be engineers so we would have a ticket to ride; mother just seemed to want us to learn stuff. We could figure out what to do with it later.

To me, her greatest legacy to her sons was that we should want—and expect—more than most rational people thought that we were entitled to, to desire without fear. Then to work to make it happen.

That's an important lesson for everybody, but probably more important for writers. What we do has no intrinsic value. Getting somebody to pay for a bunch of words is a high-flown ambition. But two of us did it. The third went another, but equally adventurous way. I think mother's philosophy applied to him as much as it did to Pat and me.

And there was one more thing: mother was one of our greatest cheerleaders. When she died, and we were going through dusty boxes in the attic, I opened one box, and it contained a history of my career, from columns in the college paper to the edition of the Benson Review I edited because Ralph and Micky were on vacation (and which contained the story of our wedding) to video scripts, ads, and several bad poems.

That's sort of what I told my brother when he asked how we got to where we were then. True then. True now.

Happy birthday, Mom.

Those who can, teach.

Last week I received a series of texts from my oldest granddaughter that, in Tin Pan Alley parlance, made the strings of my heart zing. She said that she was studying Beowulf and was "loving" the class. Then she sent a picture of her teacher in what looked like a dinosaur costume.

At first, I was puzzled. Never did I think that I would see the words "Beowulf" and "love" in close proximity. Even in translation from the original, the poem is tough going. And I couldn't figure out what Barney had to do with Beowulf. I finally decided that the costume was probably a dragon rather than a dinosaur.

But the cause of my elation was that my high-school-senior granddaughter was enthusiastic about her class, her teacher, and a 1400-year-old poem.

Here's someone who read pretty much incessantly from the time she learned to read until she got to high school. Then someone flipped a switch. She still read what she had to. She still made very good grades. But if you asked her about school, you got one of two reactions: either she didn't like it or she hated it, according to how the day had gone.

I wondered how much of this was attributable to teenage angst and how much was a rational evaluation of the instruction by a very smart young lady.

Now I'm leaning to the latter, partly because of my own experiences. In sixteen-plus years of instruction, I was blessed with a number of good teachers and a few great ones. I also endured several that treated their classes like the line at the DMV.

In the latter category was the professor I had to study Shakespeare under in college. The Bard was required, it was taught by only one professor, and by him only once a year. The professor sucked all the laughter out of the comedies and all of the spirit out of the tragedies. His only real interest was in the bones of the plays.

His tests generally consisted of about ninety quotes. We were expected to identify the act, scene, and who said it to whom.

Once I graduated I didn't read another Shakespeare play for over thirty years.

On the other side was my Modern American Poetry professor, George Herring, PhD and sometimes SOB. To say that George was eccentric would be an understatement: he threatened to resign one time because the administration had put up "Keep Off the Grass" signs. But he made the subject come alive. He was sometimes vicious in his comments on our explications, but that just made us dig in harder. George loved literature, and he loved to spark thinking about literature.

George had some advantages over normal people. He had a near-perfect memory; he seldom used notes, even on the longer poems. He had an awe-inspiring personality. If you didn't know him, you thought he was weird. If you did know him, you knew he was really weird. He had been a lot of places and done a lot of things and gave the impression that he had affected them more than they had affected him.

Now, nearly sixty years after the fact, I still remember the Modern American Poetry final. It was one sentence long: Trace the evolution of American Poetry from Whitman forward, using appropriate examples.

The final was on a Friday. He wrote the question on the board, told us that it was due by Monday noon, and we could use any resources we could find. Then he left.

There were others. Dr. Sossomon, who in a single quarter, connected the dots in more than 700 years of history. Josifina Niggli, who may well be responsible for me not spending the rest of my life flipping burgers. Mr. Wallace, who spoke a half-dozen languages and didn't seem to understand why everybody didn't. And in high school, at least two: Mrs. Lambert, who made sure that when it came to verb conjugations there would be nothing left for me to learn in college, and Judson Stephens, who terrified me to the point that I learned Algebra anyway.

For a long time, there have been arguments about teacher accountability. I, like everyone else, have opinions on that, but not enough knowledge to knew whether any of them are valid. But, from my own experience, I do know some things.

Whether students like or do not like a teacher isn't an appropriate evaluation. God knows I didn't like Mr. Stephens' algebra class, but he made it important to us. I didn't have much good to say about Mrs. Lambert's English classes either, until I found that I had a much firmer foundation in grammar than a lot of my college freshman classmates. (I went back and told her that, and she just sniffed. She knew what she was doing.)

The old saw that "those who can, do. And those who can't, teach." is a base canard. A good teacher, like a good doctor, a good writer, or a good tax attorney, can make a great difference. In fact, you could make an argument that the teacher makes a greater difference than the others.

And, finally, we do need to find a way to identify and release the teachers who phone it in, who are simply serving their time until retirement, or really don't know what they're talking about.

And we need to elevate those who are left to their proper position in our communities, rewarding them for the difference they are making.

I'm particularly grateful for the teacher in the dragon costume. Because of her, there's a chance that my granddaughter will make it through the education system without having her love for literature extinguished.

When Knowledge Exceeds Wisdom

In terms of growing old, this is—to steal from Mr. Dickens—the best of times and the worst of times. Medical science now has answers for things that sixty years ago weren't even questions. Things like genetic engineering, injections that very specifically target the bad cells in our bodies, and technology that does surgery without really cutting you.

Because of this, some of us will live longer and perhaps function better.

On the down side, technology and science have created situations that those of us who are old have difficulty understanding and dealing with. The transgendered person, for instance. Someone who was born a male and became a female or vice versa. For something like that senior citizens have no real frame of reference.

In the forties and fifties, when I was learning about the differences between male and female, we subscribed to the binary theory of gender. You were born either male or female, and you were stuck with it. We knew this to be true even though we knew that some of these gender assignments didn't seem to fit the individual they were assigned to. But it wasn't really an ethical question, a legal question, or a legislative question.

Fast forward fifty or sixty years and one of the political crises that we're faced with is whether a person who was born male and chose to become female should use the men or women's facilities in public places. Laws were passed. Meetings and conventions were canceled. And probably elections will be swayed.

And, through all of this, I was just puzzled.

Transgender rights isn't, of course, the only question. There is the on-going discussion of where treating babies for disease while they're in the womb passes into creating "designer" babies? If there's a way to make an unborn child more intelligent, is it right or wrong to do it? If we can, through machines, tubes, transplants, and other medical miracles, maintain life beyond actual living, should we do it? Or at what point should we not do it? If it's possible to create life in a petri dish, how long can we keep from actually doing it?

When I was young, questions were much less complex. Six-cylinder or V-8. Pepsi or Coke. Baptist or Methodist. There were, I'm sure, very smart people who were pondering world-changing decisions, such as what role nuclear power should have in armed conflicts. But none of that really affected me. Nobody asked my opinion, and if they had, I wouldn't have had one. But times have changed, and it appears that each of us is supposed to have an opinion, to be for or against the law, the cause, or the campaign.

So here's my solution. I will quickly concede that the person actually dealing with the problem, whether it be transgenderism, the timing and means of end of life, or curing a genetic defect before birth, is more capable of making a good decision for himself or herself that I am. And certainly more capable than a group of people essentially disconnected from the condition trying to make laws to tell them what to do.

Therefore, I support the rights of transgendered persons to use whatever bathroom they're most comfortable with. I support the rights of people facing end-of-life choices to choose the time and means for themselves. And, generally, I support the rights of each person to make the important decisions for their own life without interference from society and the government so long as it doesn't infringe on others' rights.

Certainly, there should be ethical boundaries, else we might have people choosing euthanasia over going to the office one more time. But within those broad ethical boundaries, each person should be allowed to make the choices for his or her life.

Some people may consider my attitude a copout. It may be. But I prefer to think that it's the most humane way to deal with questions that arise in a world where knowledge has far exceeded our wisdom.

Living in a Single Dimension

I am not now, nor have I ever been, black, female, gay, or Jewish. That, in my opinion, disqualifies me from defining racism, misogyny, homophobia, or anti-Semitism. I can recognize any of these, especially in their more obnoxious forms, but if a member of one of these groups tells me that they are threatened or offended by something that seems harmless enough to me, I listen.

Which makes the subject of this blog especially difficult.

It bothers me that we have been redefining people who lived in historical times not by the balance of their lives, but by a single characteristic, and that characteristic changes according to who is doing the redefining. There was a time when we could accept that sometimes people who did, by current standards, bad things could also accomplish good things.

For instance, several of my musical heroes were known to be rude and sometimes cruel people. However, I still enjoyed their music, even if I wouldn't have wanted my sister, if I'd had one, to date them. I could still recognize the brilliance of Henry Ford, even though I didn't either agree with or approve of his anti-Semitism.

And I still loved my grandfather who, by anybody's definition, was a racist. The fact was that he held the beliefs that he'd grown up with, beliefs that were sometimes at odds with his character. Just as he could get upset with me for having a black singer in one of my bands, he could close down his business to try to help a black single mother and her family. Granddaddy was a complex man, just as the world is a complex place.

What brings these ramblings on is the current debate about whether we should remember anyone as honorable men if they owned slaves. This group includes a substantial number of our founding fathers. There are people who think that owning slaves is a factor that overrides all other factors in how we judge people who lived in an entirely different time.

I believe this is dangerous.

I don't think Confederate memorials, obelisks, statues, or monuments have any place on public property, but I also don't think that everyone who fought for the Confederacy was a bad person, or even everyone who owned slaves was unmitigated evil. They lived in a time when a bad, but socially accepted institution was prevalent, and they did not fight against it.

But we judge them by today's standards.

Consider where this type of thinking will carry us. Abraham, for instance, not only owned slaves, but sexually harassed one and made her pregnant. By today's standards, his position of power would have made any contact with Hagar not only improper, but illegal. Similarly, the Lord commanded Joshua to take slaves. And keep in mind, the Jews were coming out of Egypt where they had been slaves.

None of the above is a rationalization for slavery. We know now that the ownership (or even the desire for ownership) of one person by another is reprehensible. But we also know that it took a lot of history for us to get to this point.

In 1947 there were a number of people who were judged for their thoughts and actions in a different period. Most of these people had spent their time on the side of the angels. They were opposed to racism, to the exploitation of workers, pretty much to anybody taking advantage of those less powerful. They were brought before the House Unamerican Activities committee and when they refused to answer questions because they considered them unconstitutional, they were found in contempt of Congress, fined and sentenced to prison.

They were accused of being Communists or communist sympathizers during the 1930s, and many of them were. But they were never accused of treason or attempting to overthrow the government. In fact, they were not accused of having anything less than a patriotic attitude. But they admired what the communists were attempting to do in Russia. When it was pointed out that Russia was an American ally, most of the country admired what Russia was doing in draining German military resources away from the European front, these people were accused of admiring them prematurely.

They had been convicted of having opinions that later became unpopular.

Some of the Hollywood 10 never got over the blacklist, some went underground and wrote award-winning screenplays without credit, and some were able to live through the mess. And one of the more delicious ironies of history is that the chairman of the committee, J. Parnell Thomas, was convicted of fraud and sentenced to 18 months in prison, longer than any of the Hollywood 10.

I'm not equating the black list with hundreds of years of slavery. But I am contending that people live in the context of their times, and while we may dislike or even despise some of that context, we shouldn't reduce all history to a single part of it. Life—then and now—is much more complicated than that.

Which brings me down to the argument that made me start thinking about this: was Robert E. Lee an honorable man? There have been a lot of opinions tossed back and forth. Here's mine:

In leading an army against the United States, he did, in my opinion, a dishonorable thing. It was, by definition, treasonous (as we look on it with 150 years of hindsight). But he was faced with an agonizing decision and made it. The same could be said for all the soldiers that fought under him (although most of them did not own slaves). But Grant and Lincoln thought that the objectives of the war—to reunite the country—were better served by sending these men back home. And, so far as Lee is concerned, he lived both before and after the Civil War, and in the years before he was an honored United States soldier and, in the years after, a college president. I think, like most of us, Lee was a mixed bag, both good and bad, and while I can't imagine why we'd put a statue of him in a Confederate uniform on public property, I also can't imagine why we should try to erase his name from all the things he did before and after the war.

If any member of any offended group disagrees with me, please reread paragraph one.

Falling into the Great Divide

It's hard not to feel sorry for Charlie Sykes. At least a little bit. A successful conservative radio host in Wisconsin for more than 20 years, Sykes found himself to be a man without a party, out-righted by Trump supporters. To his credit, Sykes stood up to them and took the consequences. Like many conservatives who opposed Trump, he was trolled and attacked, often maliciously.

Sykes is, by his own account, a "principled Conservative," meaning that he is in favor of small government, low taxes, and individual freedom. He appears to be thoughtful and well-read, two characteristics that Trump supporters are not noted for. He is also the author of a 2017 book entitled *How the Right Lost its Mind.* That's how I came across Sykes. I had been wondering the same thing and thought it might be useful to get a Conservative perspective.

Essentially, according to Sykes, it's a story of the White Supremacists, Evangelical leaders, and disenchanted voters who like their political philosophy distilled to bumper-strip slogans being willing to trash traditional Conservative values and join a parade behind a candidate that most of them admitted wasn't even within rock-throwing distance of those values. To anybody who has not been under a rock for the last two years, that's not news.

However, the book provides new insights into just how much pretzel twisting a lot of the better-known people had to do to rationalize their acceptance of Trump and his actions, from the leading conservative journalist who likened Trump to the chemotherapy that the country had to take to cure the cancer of liberalism to the evangelical leader who claimed Trump was a "baby Christian" who didn't have a clue about how Christians talked or what they believed, but he joined the parade. Another evangelical said: "We're electing a president, not a pastor-in-chief." In other words, character no longer matters.

The book takes a shot at explaining several things, the most important being how the United States got to the point that someone like Trump could get elected. Included in the major factors are the right-wing and the alt-right media people who promoted a state of constant outrage, building to Trump's claim that he was going to be the savior; the abandonment of fact as a basis for truth, especially at the Drudge Report, Breitbart, Fox News, and a number of lesser-known right-wing media; and—probably as the result of all of the above—the idea that the right had to save America at any cost because the election of Hillary Clinton would be a death sentence for the country.

Although I don't agree with many of Sykes' principals, I do admire his contention that we should tell the truth, that fear should not be the primary basis for running the country, and that we should promote personal responsibility. Those are principals that conservatives and liberals should be able to join together on. (Sykes wrote a list of "50 Rules that Kids Won't Learn in School," and I read the condensed version—"14 Rules Kids Won't Learn in School"—and couldn't disagree with any of them. If he wanted to go on the road preaching that message, I'd be happy to join him.)

At the end of the book, Sykes points out that there is a sliver in the Venn Diagram of traditional Conservative belief and traditional Liberal belief that overlap. He suggests that those who really want to see the country prosper and treat its citizens well work on expanding that sliver. That's also an idea I can get behind.

However, just as I was admiring much of what Sykes says in his summation, my attention went back to page 70, where he has a lengthy quote from National Review writer Charles C. W. Cooke, writing a defense of the GOP when it had been accused of "caving in to Obama." Here's the quote:

"Without the GOP manning the barricades, we'd have seen a carbon tax or cap-and-trade—or both. Without the GOP manning the barricades, we'd have got union card check, and possibly an amendment to Taft-Hartley that removed from the states their power to pass "right-to-work" exemptions. Without the GOP standing in the way, we'd now have an "assault weapons" ban, magazine limits, background checks on all private sales, and a de facto national gun registry. And without the GOP standing in the way in the House, we'd have got the very amnesty that the Trump people so fear."

From my point of view, this translates into with the Republicans manning the barricades, we're gong to live in a more polluted, more dangerous country.

The title of the National Review piece was "Against the Dangerous Myth that the GOP Has Given Obama Everything He Wanted." Given the well-documented obstructionism of the Republican Congress in the last eight years of Obama's administration, I can't help but wonder if the entire piece wasn't an exercise in gilding the obvious. However, it did remind me that I should be careful if I want to get shoulder-to-shoulder with conservatives like Charlie Sykes. They may be—and probably are—thoughtful and dedicated, but the results of their thoughtfulness and the things that they are dedicated to are often, in my opinion, bad for the country and really bad for the people of the country.

Shakespeare Made Real

I don't think about Shakespeare much. My Shakespeare professor in college essentially killed whatever fondness I had for arguably the English language's greatest writer. But since last night I have been fixated on Sonnet 73 (*This time of year thou mayst in me behold/ When yellow leaves, or none, or few, do hang/ upon the boughs which shake against the cold/ bare ruin'd choirs, where late the sweet birds sang.*) I learned last night that one of my childhood friends had been moved to a nursing home.

Yesterday was his birthday, and we had tried to call him to give him birthday greetings. His phone had been disconnected. We called a mutual friend to see if we could learn what was going on and found that he had been moved to the nursing home because he could no longer live alone.

The last time we talked, he was in a wheelchair, but could carry on an energetic conversation. Now, I'm told, he drifts off during a conversation. I couldn't help but think of the "yellow leaves, where none or few do hang," dead leaves but not yet fallen.

My friend's life, like most, was a mixed bag of the good and the bad with a bit of the terrible. In his case, both the good and the bad seemed amplified. On the good side were his creative gifts. He was a fine, if eccentric, pianist. He could, I suppose, read music, but he chose not to. He played everything by ear, and usually solo, because the only key he would play in was five

209

flats. Later, after his divorce, he would put this to work, playing cocktail piano in hotel bars. Probably always in D-flat.

He was also an excellent chef and served as executive chef for a large tech company. When we last talked he was still proud of his culinary skills.

He did a lot of things well, but there was a sad thread that ran through his life from beginning to end. Part of this consisted of things that were nobody's business, but his. Another part was the breakup of his marriage and the estrangement of one of his two daughters. He thought it ironic that the daughter who was still speaking to him lived in Connecticut, and the one wasn't speaking to him lived in the town where he lived. The undercurrent of our last conversation was that he had essentially been left alone. His family, including his younger sister, had died, and his wife and one of the two daughters were, to put it quaintly, distant.

We talked about him getting back to some of the things he loved. He had an easel and paints. He had a keyboard, and someone had offered to set it up for him. He was working on something he hoped to be an op-ed piece for the Times. There was, we thought, still time to do something that, although it might not be important, would be pleasurable.

I doubt any of these things were done. There wasn't really any more time.

I don't know why his move to the nursing home struck me so hard. We had been good friends, but we went separate ways, and I don't think we had talked more than a half-dozen times in the last fifty years. We were no longer an important part of each other's lives.

Part of it is, I think, the sorrow of a life with so much promise ending so sadly, living alone in a small house until he was no longer capable of living there. It was not enough to be talented and creative.

Another part of it is that we were young together, and now we're both old. His situation is not foreign to any of us who once thought we had so much future and had it speed by while we were living our lives.

But I think the biggest part of bothers me is that I don't know what to pray for for him. Peace. Grace. Feeling the love of God. He won't get well, and I doubt that in this world the scars that the bad things left on him will heal.

The third quatrain of the sonnet pretty well sums it up: *In me thou see'st the glowing of such fire/That on the ashes of his youth doth lie,/As the death-bed whereon it must expire,/Consum'd with that which it was nourish'd by.*

His phone's been disconnected. I'm sorry. I would like to at least tell him that Linda and I care about him.

Betsy DeVos gives me hope.

Like most people, I have opinions about how to improve our public schools. Unlike many, because I have friends who are professional educators and know a lot more about it than I do, I have been reluctant to voice those opinions. However, since the appointment of Betsy DeVos as Secretary of Education, I have become emboldened. Evidently, it is now acceptable for someone with no education credentials to have a serious influence on our public schools.

Admittedly, I don't have the single education credential that Betsy DeVos claims: I did not fund the program that took one of the worst school systems in the country and made it worse, reducing or eliminating accountability for the charter schools that she was pushing for. However, I do have some relevant experience: I have for years created accountability systems for sales and management; I have designed dozens of programs to train business people; I have developed a system for measuring the ROI of training (the training itself, not just the delivery systems); and I spent a lot of years being judged by adults who sat in and paid for my seminars.

Still, I am not a professional educator, and I imagine most of them will disagree with what I'm about to say.

First, the big issue: teacher accountability. It's always been strange to me that teachers in schools with large resources are being compared to teachers in schools with scant resources. One of the tenets of sales accountability is that we have to reduce the number of variables if we want to measure the output of the employee. In most cases, we simply indexed them. Sales people were ranked according to how well they met the company's sales objectives. This eliminated conversations like the following:

Salesperson: I know I didn't make my budget. I can't do that when our prices are too high, and our inventory is too low.

Manager: You're ninth out of nine salespeople. They're all dealing with the same market, the same prices, and the same inventory you are.

So, my first accountability point is that teachers be compared only to others in the same school, dealing with the same kinds of students, and—probably at least as important—with the same kinds of parents.

Next, I would change the measurement protocol. I don't think (and some of my professional educator friends would agree with me) that standardized tests are the best way of measuring student progress. It's a very narrow measurement, focusing on the retention and regurgitation of some material. Part of my disdain for standardized tests is—and this may be surprising—that I always do very well on them. I have an interesting, but essentially useless talent for taking standardized tests. The upside of that is that it gave me something to brag about; the downside was that all of the college departments wanted me until they found that I wasn't as advertised.

The measurement protocol that I would suggest involves changing the definition of success in the teacher's job. My definition of the teacher's job would be that the teacher prepares the student for success in the next level. Up until the senior year that means the next grade. In the senior year, that means preparation for college or the work world.

This is measured not by the students' grades or scores at the end of the year, but at the end of either one or two grades higher, the idea being that we eliminate differences in specific class cohorts by letting them be scatted among other teachers in the next grade. Whether the measurement for the fourth grade is at the end of the fifth grade or the sixth grade should be subject to study.

This system reduces a large number of variables: concentration of good students in a single class, the positive bias for good test takers, the availability of resources, and the level of parent involvement. And for reasons that I probably don't know, it may be totally unworkable.

My next suggestion has to do with conforming public education to the world we live in. Last year, a Georgia legislator complained that students probably weren't remembering facts; they were probably Googling them. It seemed that he thought that it was important for the student to memorize that the Norman Conquest happened in 1066, a fact they can pull off the web in seconds. I think it's more important for the student to be able to clearly and concisely state the impact of the Norman Conquest on the world we live in today. Consequently, I would suggest that grades 1-8 be devoted to vocabulary and basic skills, (e.g., the parts of speech, how to write a paragraph, math problems, reading, etc.). High school courses would concentrate on having the students use those skills in critical thinking and problem solving.

(If a student manages to get out of junior high without the basic skills, say the ability to make subjects and verbs agree, I think there should be short remediation programs available online for the student. The teacher doesn't stop to deal with what should have been dealt with last year or the year before.)

Which leads to my final and most controversial suggestion, especially for an English major: I think we should abandon the four-year requirement for literature and that all literature courses should be electives for those who enjoy that sort of thing. In their place I think there should be eight or maybe twelve credit hours—two-hour or three-hour classes for four years—in a course entitled "Culture," which combines the politics, history, music, art, and economics of specified periods in a single class. It is, for instance, easier to appreciate some of the plays of Shakespeare if you understand the class divisions and economics of Elizabethan England and that he had to entertain both the literate and illiterate at the same time. The Culture class would provide a broad (if superficial) study of everything that had an impact on the time.

(Again, full disclosure: I have always contended that my life was not measurably improved by memorizing broad swaths of Macbeth in the 10th grade. That time might have been better spent trying to connect the dots on important things that happened in the 16th or 17th century, some of which may have included the production of Macbeth.)

Although any or all these ideas may well be ignored by people who know more than I do about these things, I figured if Betsy DeVos, who couldn't even answer basic questions at her confirmation hearings, can be a power in education, I can try to be, too.

(For my article, All Training is not Basic Training, in which I explain why we shouldn't spend all our time on basic skills, such as how to build a bomb, without moving to more critical-thinking skills, such as figuring out who should be bombed, visit corstrat.org.)

&

Why the Gun Rights People Should Fear the Children

There have been a variety of reactions to the student walkouts over the Parkland, Florida school shooting. Many people have been supportive, understanding that students are rightfully concerned for their own safety and the safety of others. Many have just ignored it, preferring to give their attention to more personal or more pressing concerns. And some have been dismissive, saying that these are kids who don't know enough to protest or, even worse, that their concerns are not sincere, that they are "crises actors."

Those are the ones who should be very afraid. Their brand of arrogance mixed with lethal doses of ignorance may well cause them to lose much more than what the children are asking for. Right now, their demands—if they can be called such—is that the adults in charge do their jobs and help secure their safety. It's not a big ask, no more than any citizen young or old should expect.

But we have a variety of autocratic responses, from school authorities promising suspension to students who participate in the protest to the NRA's suit against the state of Florida for raising the age limit for purchasing AR-15s. Essentially, these people are telling the students to sit down and shut up. Children should be seen and not heard.

There have already be parallels drawn between the protests triggered by the Parkland shooting and the student protests of the civil rights movement and the anti-war protests of the late sixties. Both of these had far reaching effects beyond what the protesters were asking for when they started. The first brought about the Civil Rights Act of 1964. The second brought down the president, the same president who signed the Civil Rights Act.

Both protests brought about major change and were led by students. That should be enough evidence to cause people to take the Parkland students and the students around the country who protested in solidarity with them seriously. But, again, adults are sometimes handicapped by arrogance, a lack of appreciation for history, tunnel vision, or just plain stupidity.

And they may try to point out some differences in the civil rights and anti-war protests and the current protests. The earlier ones were led by adults and college students. High school students did participate, but the focus was on the older people. They were massive (although the point might be made that having thousands of students across the country walk out in a coordinated protest qualifies as massive). And at least the anti-war protest was reflecting a majority opinion in the country (although it's been reported that a majority of Americans are for tighter gun restrictions, background checks, and even the return of the 1994 ban on semi-automatic weapons).

For these people, I'd like to introduce Barbara Rose Johns, late of Prince Edward County, Virginia.

In 1951 Barbara Johns was a 16-year-old black student, by all evidence bright and ambitious. Her later career as an activist bears this out. However, as a student, Barbara didn't think that she and her fellow students were getting as good an education as Virginia could offer.

Barbara's sister describes the Robert R. Moton High School like this:

"The school we went to was overcrowded. Consequently, the county decided to build three tarpaper shacks for us to hold classes in. A tarpaper shack looks like a dilapidated black building, which is similar to a chicken coop on a farm. It's very unsightly. In winter the school was very cold. And a lot of times we had to put on our jackets. Now, the students that sat closest to the wood stove were very warm and the ones who sat farthest away were very cold. And I remember being cold a lot of times and sitting in the classroom with my jacket on. When it rained, we would get water through the ceiling. So there were lots of pails sitting around the classroom. And sometimes we had to raise our umbrellas to keep the water off our heads. It was a very difficult setting for trying to learn."

There was a newer, better, all-white school across town. The students at the Robert R. Moton High School knew it was there. They knew it was better equipped. And that the students didn't have to get an education in spite of the conditions. This was in a state that publicly said that it provided "separate, but equal education," and privately held that since the blacks didn't pay a lot of taxes, the state didn't owe them a lot. It had been this way for years, and so far as the white citizens of Prince Edward County were concerned, it would always be this way.

However, Barbara Johns had other ideas. She recruited the best and brightest in her high school (the president of the student body, the senior class president, and others) and they spent six months formulating a plan. According to one account, they met in a concrete building beneath the football stands and called their effort "the Manhattan Project." When they had completed their plan, they lured the principal away from the school (so that he wouldn't be punished for being complicit), called an assembly (barring the teachers from entering it, so that they wouldn't be punished for being complicit), and Barbara Johns made a speech. According to her sister, the assembly went like this:

"She walked up to the podium and she started to tell everyone about the fact that she wanted us to cooperate with her because the school was going out on a strike. I remember sitting in my seat and trying to go as low in the seat as I possibly could because I was so shocked and so upset. I actually was frightened because I knew that what she was doing was going to have severe consequences. I didn't know what they were going to be, but I knew there were going to be some. She stood up there and addressed the school. She seemed to have everyone's attention.... At one point, she took off her shoe and she banged on the podium and said that we were going to go out on strike and would everyone please cooperate and 'don't be afraid, just follow us out.' So we did. The entire student body followed her out."

They marched down to the superintendent's office, and Barbara told him that they lived in the modern world and wanted to be educated for it, that they wanted an education like the white students were getting. The superintendent threatened them with expulsion, and when they didn't work, he threatened to have their parents arrested. A student pointed out that the jail wasn't big enough to hold all their parents.

Because the superintendent simply dismissed the students' concerns, that meeting was the beginning rather than the end of the effort. There were meetings. There was a cross burning. There were economic reprisals. But the students didn't give up.

Barbara Johns had to leave the county because her family feared for her safety, but the protest that she started became the largest and the only student-led case of the six suits that were folded into Brown v. Board of Education. That decision rendered "equal education" moot because it made "separate" education illegal.

Barbara Johns and her fellow students might well have been satisfied with a decent building, new books, and a chance to learn without having to be so obviously second-class citizens, but those in power dismissed their concerns, and the whole world of education was changed. Even after Brown v. the Board of Education, Virginia tried a number of maneuvers to avoid integration, including shutting down all public schools and promoting a plan to privatize education. Sort of an early version of Betsy DeVos' plans. However, between the people in Virginia who felt that integration was wrong and the people who felt that defying what the court had made the law of the land was wrong, Virginia finally came around. It took a while, but Barbara Johns and her schoolmates won much more than they originally asked for.

The gun-rights people should take a lesson from this. If you dismiss the children and their concerns, you may end up with much less than you would have had if you'd paid attention. Remember, they'll be here long after we're gone.

Happy Mother's Day

It was a strange place to find inspiration for a Mother's Day blog: the Lincoln Center Essentially Ellington competition.

I've written blogs about my mother and my children's mother, both of whom have been very important to me. I've written about my grandchildren's mother, who's important to them and to me. But this year I was at a loss.

Until I watched part of the Essentially Ellington competition.

For those who missed it, this is an annual competition of high school jazz bands playing the works of Duke Ellington. They are amazing. Any one of them is better than any of the swing bands I've played in, and they're still improving.

But the thing that struck me is the women (girls, females, whatever your favorite term is) in those bands. Several of the bass players were female, including one whose bass was probably a foot taller than she was, even in heels. In one band three of the four trumpets were female. In another, there was a person of the female persuasion on bari sax. One of the really swinging piano players was a girl. There were several female trombone players. They were scattered throughout all of the sections, just as if they were real jazz musicians. And they were.

At this point, you may be wondering what I'm prattling about and why. And what does any of this have to do with Mother's Day.

First, I was in my sixties before I ever played alongside a female musician in a swing band. We usually had what was called a "girl singer," but the horns and the rhythm section was considered male territory.

This led me to wonder how much better some of those bands might have been if we hadn't thought that only males could play swing and jazz. What had gender stereotypes cost us? Probably a lot.

And it goes a lot wider than just big bands. When Linda told me she was going to work, I pronounced that no wife of mine would work outside the home. Like most of my pronouncements, it was not only wrong but ignored. She went to work, still did what she was supposed to do as a mother, and became a nurse.

It wasn't an either/or situation. It was the ability to do both well. My mother did the same thing. She worked from the time I was six. She still did all of her motherly and wifely duties. Now my daughter is using the degree she worked so hard for in a job that seems to give her a good deal of satisfaction. And she's still doing her motherly and wifely duties.

I was raised in an era when the received wisdom was that a woman's place was in the home. It was more talk than fact even them. Farm wives were at the barn at sun up, had dinner on the table at noon, and kept the house clean. Women worked in offices and stores. They even voted.

Yet society still operated on what appears to be a male view of the female life. We were, are, and always have been sexist. Else there would be no need for feminism.

The received wisdom was that the man was the breadwinner, the woman the homemaker, and to try to be anything else was—at least—sinful.

It's not that I don't think motherhood is an important job. It may be, in fact, the most important job. But fatherhood is important, too, and nobody suggests that men should only be fathers, and not salespeople, lawyers, writers, doctors, etc.

Today I want to celebrate the mothers who have been important to me. My mother. My children's mother. My grandchildren's
mother. My mother-in-law (who almost always took my side if
Linda and I had an argument). And all the other mothers who try
to raise their children to upstanding, decent, people, sometimes
in the face of stiff societal resistance. I want to thank them for
doing their motherly, and wifely duties and still contributing
outside the home.

And I wish them the fullest life they can have, unrestrained
by what men thought that women should be.

It seems that we've been very wrong before.

Father's Day in Perspective

For most of my life, Mother's Day has been a larger holiday than Father's Day. Before direct-dial long distance, there was always a newspaper story about Mother's Day having the highest call volume of any day of the year. There was never a story about the number of people calling Dad.

And there were usually more ads suggesting gifts for Mom than for Dad on their special days. It seemed that by all measures, Mother's Day was a bigger blast than Father's Day.

And that seemed to be the natural order of things. I mean, whoever heard of a father lion attacking to defend his cubs. It's always the mother.

It's only been in my old age that I realized that macro-statistics and retail attention really don't say much about the importance of Father's Day. I don't think I ever resented the day's second-class status, but if I did, I know that I was wrong. The important part of Father's Day happened every year.

My children—and now my grandchildren—recognized that I had been a part of their lives, and they said that they were grateful.

That, to me, is as good as it needs to get.

I hope I communicated that to my dad. I'm not sure, because his birthday was usually just days away from Father's Day; he got an all-purpose gift to cover both days, and I don't remember including my thanks to him for all that he had done for me while I was growing up. He not only taught me the subtleties of baseball, but he provided a living example of what a real man was. If we had been Jewish, he would have been a mensch.

He did not ask for much, and he gave all that he could. He and mother raised three boys and provided them with opportunities far beyond their means. There was something Sisyphean about Dad's life. For as long as could remember, he (and a multitude of other fathers) got up every morning and put their shoulder to the stone, knowing that after the end that week, there would come the beginning of another with exactly the same challenges.

I'm no poet, but years ago, I was moved to write what I passed off as a poem about this. It's entitled "When the Eagle Flaps Its Wings." For those who don't recognize the phrase, it's the cleaned-up version of a slang term for payday. Since Dad did not curse or use vulgarities, this is the version he always used. The poem is on the next page.

Happy Father's Day to all the fathers who got up every morning and did one more thing to make the lives of their families better, along with the hope that they recognize that good children grown to good adults are the best of Father's Day gifts.

§

When the Eagle Flaps Its Wings

On a Saturday, a little after noon,
Eleanor passed out the envelopes.
Skinny brown envelopes
only a little wider than a dollar bill
and not much thicker.
He'd take the envelope,
put the change in his pocket,
the bills in his wallet,
and start down Main St,
to the grocery store every week,
to the dry goods store most every week,
and to the cleaners, the drug store,
and the hardware store
when it was their turn.
It seemed like a long walk,
and there was always too much Main Street.
But everybody greeted him, talked about
the crops and the weather, and asked
about the family
because they knew who he was,
and who his mama and daddy were,
and they knew that every week,
the eagle flapped its wings.

Won't You Be My Neighbor?

Yesterday, Linda and I and our children took a long stroll down distant-memory lane and saw the documentary about Fred Rogers and his neighborhood. Our little group was representative of the entire audience, older people and middle-aged people, the children who had watched Mr. Rogers and the parents who let them.

The documentary had as much to do with why Fred Rogers created the neighborhood as it did the man himself. Rogers was an ordained Presbyterian minister who felt a particular calling to children. He saw the sort of messages children's shows were delivering—violence, violence disguised as comedy, and violence disguised as human accidents—and determined that those weren't the messages that children needed to be hearing.

(Our own children watched Mr. Rogers in the morning and the Popeye Club in the afternoon. In the Popeye Club, the hero frequently saved his girlfriend by slugging Bluto.)

Admittedly, I was a little leery of Mr. Rogers back then. Here was this quiet guy who came through the door singing, immediately took off his coat, and put on a sweater. Then he changed shoes and fed the fish. I didn't watch the program that closely. Now, having seen the movie, I wish I had.

Rogers had one overriding theme that had nothing to do with changing clothes or feeding fish. It was simply this: Every child deserves to expect and receive love, no matter who that child is.

That would seem to be a wallowing in the obvious, not something to base a number of years of successful children's shows on. Of course, that wasn't all that he said. He made pointed statements on current themes, such as the fight over the segregation of public swimming pools, the assassination of Robert Kennedy, and the Challenger explosion. But even as he treated these incidents, there was the lesson he kept teaching: children are loved and will be kept safe by the adults around them.

And a part of that was that children who were different deserved the same thing.

There were several places in the movie where I teared up, but the one that got me the most was when a child paralyzed because of surgery to remove a spinal tumor and confined to a wheel chair was brought to the neighborhood just before he was to have surgery to fuse his spine. His parents knew that the surgery was necessary, but that their son might not make it. Rogers talked calmly with the boy about why he was in a wheel chair and what they were going to do. Then they sang a song together: I like you just the way you are.

That's when the tears escaped from my eyes and rolled down my cheeks. I think that's something every child needs to hear.

Earlier this week, Facebook resurrected one of my posts from some years ago. It was an almost-poem entitled "Free Expression."

> Day by day, expectations
> wrap themselves ever more tightly
> around me until
> I'm just a bundle of what everyone else
> thinks I should be.
> But one day I'll shed that cocoon of expectation
> and be just who I am.

When I wrote that, I thought that this was about as good as it got, that we'd live long enough and be strong enough to one day shed the expectations of others and be what the psychologists call our "authentic" self. But Mr. Rogers thought differently. He thought that we should accept people as and where they are, rather than imposing our expectations and judgments on them.

I think he was right.

I was thoroughly enjoying the movie until about fifteen minutes from the end. Some talking heads, self-proclaimed experts, and generally nasty people started attacking Mr. Rogers and his love-'em-like-they-are philosophy. One was shown saying that Rogers was contributing to the downfall of the country by trying to convince all children that they were special. Another said that this was the attitude that had created a generation of young adults who felt entitled. Some shrill TV wench was shouting that he was an "evil, evil man."

And that made me very sad. These people had taken neither the time nor trouble to understand what Rogers were saying, but even worse, they had hijacked his message to fit their narrative. In effect, they were denying that it was our responsibility to love and protect our children, to accept their imperfections and love them still. We're hearing a lot of that today.

Then there was the final insult.

When Mr. Rogers died, the Westboro Baptist Church demonstrated at his funeral. Not in favor of his example of Christian love and concern for his fellow man, but to disrupt the last service for someone they felt accepted gays.

(If you go to the Westboro Baptist web site, you'll see their message: God hates fags and other proud sinners.)

229

But these people, like the haters on TV, had badly missed the point. Fred Rogers did indeed accept and love gay people. One of them testified to that in the movie. But that wasn't the point.

Fred Rogers accepted everyone just as they are. And just as the Christ he followed did.

The documentary couldn't have come out at a better time.

Civility and Its Tragic Death

Once upon a time, I wanted to be a mathematician. However, I quickly proved, as I had with music and chemistry, that I didn't really have talent in that field. However, these many years later I have defined what I think is a law that spans a host of specific areas of the world we live in:

The decline in civility is inversely proportionate to the increase in stupidity.

This will be henceforth known as Holmes' Law on the Death of Rational Debate.

It's been going on for a while, ever since people discovered that it was easier simply to call somebody a pejorative name than to actually bring facts to an argument. But, like Typhoid Mary's typhoid, it lived beneath the surface. It was there but not so obvious to really disturb the host. It was until recently we seemed to become proud of it.

There are, for instance, a lot of comments on the web about political correctness. In fact, some people seem to think that political correctness will be the death of civilization as we know it. We have a gubernatorial candidate that seems to pride himself on being politically incorrect.

Because of what I've done for a living for so many years, I'm something of an expert on the uses and abuses of political correctness. During the seventies and eighties, you needed a five-foot bookshelf of PC rules and regulations. And some of those rules and regulations were just silly:

He or she should immediately make an appointment with his or her OB/GYN.

Or the fact that in a script a woman should never be shown as a housewife. (That one caused me to rewrite several scripts of instructional television after some militant PC folks got hold of them.)

But behind each of these nonsensical rules, there was a real and important consideration.

The stories that we told were not always about a "he." For hundreds of years, the generic pronoun for the population was the masculine one. I can see how, if I were of the feminine persuasion, that would bother me. So we ended up with tortured sentence constructions while we tried to figure out what grammatical gender equality looked like.

And the woman should not always be shown as a housewife. In those years we went from Father Knows Best and Leave it to Beaver to Mary Tyler Moore and Murphey Brown. None of those models were wrong, but neither were any of them always right.

However, that's not what the anti-PC folks seem to be about. They want to be able to call all Muslims terrorists, all immigrants rapists, and all people who think differently from them by names such as snowflakes, libtards, or (gasp) liberals. In my opinion, that has nothing to do with political correctness. It's just being a jerk, and worse, it's being stupid.

It's a matter of fact that all Muslims aren't terrorists; they've been living among us for generations without stirring up fear. And it's a matter of fact that the crime rate among those not born here is actually lower than among those born here. However, it doesn't serve the needs of those who need their constituency to be afraid to deal with that. It's easier to characterize whole populations as law breakers.

And the same sort of thing is already showing up in the Georgia governor's race. We're being treated to a steady diet of PAC-sponsored commercials that characterize the Democratic candidate as "radical, fiscally irresponsible, and unqualified."

Never do the commercials attempt to show what policies she promotes could be considered radical. They do make much of the fact that she has a payment plan to pay some back taxes, about $54,000 worth according to the commercial. If she filed her taxes on time (and she says she did), Stacey Abrams took perfectly legal steps to deal with a cash shortage. We should all be so honorable.

As has been reported, the Republican candidate has refused to honor about $500,000 in personally guaranteed loans made to a company in which he was involved. The loans are past due, and Rick Phillips, the guy who loaned Hart AgStrong the money says he would like to get paid. Kemp says that he will not speak to that.

Which brings us back to civility and stupidity.

It takes a couple of minutes to get beneath the charges to the facts of the matter

But, we don't want to or feel the need to get beneath the charges. We like the charges. We're comfortable with them. We're addicted to confirmation bias.

You can almost see the brain cells popping and deflating.

And it will only get worse.

Those of us who are old enough will remember a time when being called a liar was a serious insult. Now, when caught in a lie, people tell another to cover it up.

We remember when we prided ourselves in being courteous. It was the sign of a civilized person. But now we not only sit on our horns at stoplights, measuring the smallest unit of time between the light change and the honk, but we feel free to call names, impugn motives, and spread lies. And we do it in increasing volume.

I am a liberal, consequently, most of the examples cited here show the shallowness of some conservatives. However, a thoughtful conservative could well match me example for example.

And that's a part of the tragedy of the situation.

Our Peculiar Institution

Recently, my 11-year-old grandson told me that they were study-ing the Civil War. Although I'm not a big fan of the Civil War, I wanted to be an attentive grandfather, so I asked him what he had learned.

"That it wasn't over slavery," he said. "It was over state's rights."

After reminding him that his primary job was to get to the sixth grade in good order and that there was little to be gained by debating with his teacher (or trying to make an argument on a test), I told him that I disagreed with that version and that—so far as I was concerned—it was one of two or three revisionist theories that attempt to either sanitize southern history or demonize it.

He appeared to accept what I said, or at least he didn't choose to debate it.

Then, last week when I was combing through *The Sing* to see how many inconsistencies and typos we had missed in the first five proofings, I came upon this:

> *River Falls became a town just a few years after the end of what some people still called "the War of Northern Aggression." The people there had been involved in the war on battlefields as far away as Pennsylvania and as close as their own farms. They weren't fighting to keep their slaves; there were only a few holdings in the county large enough to either need or support them. The largest landowner in what became River Falls made do by having a dozen children. But the farmers did see the need*

to fight because it seemed like somebody was trying to change the
way they lived. And they resisted that on principal.

For a moment, I was confused. I knew both of these things—
what I had told Quinn and what I had written— to be true, but
at first glance, they appeared to be contradictory. But that lasted
only for a moment, because the seeming contradiction was cleared
up by one of the great truths of national warfare: The people
in power start the war, then leave it to others to fight and die
in it. The fact was that most of the soldiers who fought for the
Confederacy didn't come from plantations; they came from small
farms. And they weren't fighting to keep the slaves that they had
never had; they were fighting because they had been told that
they must to keep what they did have.

It was also a fact that, for the most part, people who worried
about such a thing accepted that the War was about slavery. That's
especially true of the politicians. In 1837, John C. Calhoun delivered a speech entitled "Speech on the Reception of Abolition
Petitions," in which he said that the abolitionists were tearing the
country apart. He also said:

> *I appeal to facts. Never before has the black race of Central*
> *Africa, from the dawn of history to the present day, attained a*
> *condition so civilized and so improved, not only physically, but*
> *morally and intellectually. It came among us in a low, degraded,*
> *and savage condition, and in the course of a few generations*
> *it has grown up under the fostering care of our institutions,*
> *reviled as they have been to its present comparatively civilized*
> *condition. This, with the rapid increase of numbers, is conclusive*
> *proof of the general happiness of the race, in spite of all the*
> *exaggerated tales to the contrary.*

Yet, there were prominent people throughout the South who
said that if the slave population wasn't forcefully held down, they'd

rise up and kill the whites. (In 1848, the Baptists were asked if it was Christian to beat slaves. After due deliberation, the Baptists concluded it was.)

In this case, the points of contention (and the aims of the Abolitionists) were banning slavery in the District of Columbia and prohibiting slave trade across state lines. Thirteen years later, when he was too ill to deliver it, Calhoun had a colleague read what is remembered by historians as his most famous speech. Near the end he says:

> *Unless something decisive is done, I again ask, What is to stop this agitation before the great and final object at which it aims--the abolition of slavery in the States--is consummated? Is it, then, not certain that if something is not done to arrest it, the South will be forced to choose between abolition and secession? Indeed, as events are now moving, it will not require the South to secede in order to dissolve the Union. Agitation will of itself effect it, of which its past history furnishes abundant proof--as I shall next proceed to show.*

At this point, South Carolina had already threatened succession once and had advanced something called the "Nullification Doctrine," which held that states could nullify any federal law that it didn't agree with.

For years, much of the energy of the legislative branch (and some of the energy of the judicial branch) was spent trying to hold the Union together. They passed the Missouri Compromise, which accepted Maine into the union along with Missouri. In 1857, the Supreme Court ruled that an African-American could not be a citizen and had no standing to sue. When the Kansas-Nebraska act opened the territories for settlement, pro-slavery settlers and anti-slavery settlers poured in, hoping to determine slavery's future in the state.

Politicians spent a lot of time on the South's so-called "peculiar institution." Which might strike some future researchers as odd, considering that most Southerners did not have a dog in this particular fight. Estimates of the number of southerners who owned slaves range from 5% to 30%. In any case, it was such a minority that the South could not have gone to war if only slave holders were fighting. So those who owned slaves found a way to make those who didn't willing to fight. It was fear of loss. Loss of life. Loss of status. Loss of opportunity.

Pretty much the same thing that happens today.

All my life I've been told that blacks want something I have. I've also been told how dangerous they are. And how they'll take our jobs. It's never said, but at the base of it all is the fear that they'll take our status. If we have no one to look down on, where will we be.

And, I think, that's the biggest fear that the slave-owning population used to get the people of my home county to fight and die for something that primarily benefitted the rich.

In 150 years, we've learned very little.

This is what we've come to.

In his book, *Costly Grace*, subtitled "An Evangelical Minister's Rediscovery of Faith, Hope, and Love," Rob Schenck tells about a presentation from a fundraising group who was promoting "Fear and Anger" as their primary motivator. They told him that if he presented his plans and the benefits the plans would bring, some people would send him some money, but if he aroused their fears and stoked their anger, they would send him a lot of money.

I'm sure Schenck recognized the ironic parallel between "Fear and Anger" of the fundraisers and his own group: Faith and Action. And I'm sure that he recognized the inflammatory language that his anti-abortion group had used in Operation Rescue as an excellent example of it.

But I doubt that he realized that over the next twenty years, it would become the way we do politics. It seems that fear and anger is as effective for gathering votes as it is for raising money. And the most prominent example of it was the Donald Trump campaign.

An observant person could get whiplash from trying to keep up with whom we're supposed to be afraid of on any given day. It was probably one of the following:

- Mexicans because they are coming to take our jobs, rape our women, and turn the country brown.
- Muslims because beneath every burqa is a suicide vest and in every mosque a terror cell.

239

- Democrats because they are dragging us down the slippery slope to socialism and/or communism.
- Secularists are turning our nation into a bunch of atheists, and if we don't become a theocracy God is going to get us.
- Feminists are persecuting males, and males must fight back before they lose their position.
- Blacks are taking the country away from the whites.

That's just a partial list, but it's sufficient to show that we are not being led. We're being manipulated. It seems that just as everybody is afraid of something, there is somebody who wants to use it as a wedge or a hammer to cause that person to join the flock.

I have a good deal of difficulty believing any of this. I know that this country is still roughly two-thirds white, 70% self-identified Christian, and that 75% of the senior executives in US companies are male. If you limit the range to CEOs of Fortune 500 companies, the figure is higher than 90%. If you look at the number of black CEOs in those companies, the figure is almost zero. As an old, Christian, white male, I have some difficulty knowing who I should be afraid of or why I should be afraid. Seems like, of all the people in this country, I and my particular tribe should be the most secure.

Now I'm watching the Trump campaign being recreated on a more inept level by the Republican candidate for governor of Georgia. Last night during what is every more accurately denoted as "fringe time" on television, I was treated to three commercials calling Stacey Abrams "too extreme for Georgia." According to the commercials, she has allied herself with pedophiles and "government-run health care."

And I've seen both of these claims repeated on social media. Shows that some people prefer to be manipulated by "fear and anger" than to do ten minutes of research.

The sex offender bill that Abrams voted against was, in the eyes of a number of legislators and non-partisan organizations, simply bad law. It substituted a very specific list of places prohibited to sexual offenders for a broader provision in the existing law. The existing law said that convicted sexual predators were prohibited from being within 1000 feet from where children congregate.

Essentially Stacy Abrams vote was to maintain a blanket ban rather create a list of specific places, with the high probability that some place where children congregate might be overlooked..

It would also seem that if you're going to use that vote to paint Stacey Abrams as a friend to pedophiles, you would need to include the 30 other Georgia legislators who voted the same way.

It was, as with a lot of other legislation these days, a bit of show business that at the surface and to some people sounds good, but when more closely examined is shown to accomplish nothing.

And, of course, that vote was ten years ago.

The "government-run healthcare" claim evidently comes from Abrams platform plank saying she will try to expand Medicaid in Georgia. The result will be better, more available healthcare for a state that has the highest rate of pregnancy-related deaths in the nation and ranks 43rd in the nation in overall health care. Abrams is recommending the same thing that the majority of states, including Republican-led states, have already implemented.

Nothing in her platform seems the least bit extreme, socialistic or communistic to me. You can read it for yourself at https://staceyabrams.com/issues/. If you really want to feel wonkish, also visit Brian Kemp's website and compare their platforms.

Then you can ignore all the attempts at fear and anger aimed at you every night on your TV.

We have, as so many have already pointed out, become a nation of snowflakes or—probably more accurate—a nation of timid birds scared by every scarecrow that those with money and power want to put in front of us.

I'm old enough to remember when we bravely took on big challenges and often succeeded. That's one part of our past I'd like bring back.

What we've come to makes me very sad.

The Sadness that We Have Become

This past week more than a dozen pipe bombs were mailed to Democratic leaders, including an ex-president and an ex-vice-president, several members of Congress and various others who had been critical of Trump.

Yesterday, a man walked into a synagogue during services and gunned down 11 worshipers.

It would be helpful if we could be more than shocked at these things, if we could be surprised that such a thing could happen in the United States. It would be better if we could say, as the people interviewed on television in front of crime scenes at a residence say, that you'd never expect something like this to happen in such a quiet country.

But we can't say that. This has become our existence.

Trump said that it would have probably been better if there had been an armed guard inside the synagogue, that he might have been able to kill the shooter before he killed 11 others. Perhaps, or perhaps there would be one more dead, this one with a gun in his hand or holster.

This is the sadness we have become.

Where we have to have an armed guard to prevent a slaughter while we have a ceremony to name a baby. Where the answer to death by gunfire is more gunfire, and probably more death.

This country has never been a particularly peaceful place for all of its citizens. In the years after the Civil War, about 4,000 blacks were lynched in the formerly Confederate states. About 1,000 people were killed in labor disputes. Since the 1920s, more than 50 black churches were burned, bombed, or vandalized. There were more than 6,000 reported hate crimes last year, many against blacks, Muslims, and LGBT people. (Note that these are reported hate crimes. 92 large cities didn't report any at all.)

We have traditionally found groups who, in the minds of some of our citizens, should be targets rather than neighbors.

But now it's different. Even when I was young, and the south had institutionalized its racism through Jim Crow laws, violence was not so commonplace. Nor was there the perceived need to protect our schools and churches with armed guards. Nobody marched in the streets with long guns to intimidate their neighbors.

It appears that we've given up to violence and senseless death as the new normal. We do not have the unity, the will, nor the leadership to make our country safe. Instead, we say that we need more guns to protect us from the guns, and I suppose it follows that we need better bombs to protect us from the bombers.

In the 1950s there were several movies that used doors with a ridiculous number of locks as a comic device. In the 21st century, that's no longer funny.

Trump said that shootings such as the one that happened yesterday are happening here and "around the world." That may be a fact, but it's not a truth. We seem to be the champions in the sport of killing our citizens because we don't like them. We average more than one mass shooting a day in this country. For comparison purposes, consider all of Europe: 34 shootings in all of 2016, and more than half of those were in Russia and the Ukraine.

I remember a dystopian movie from years ago where the hero was walking down a badly lit street, looking over his shoulder, wondering where the danger was coming from. The street was empty, but he was certain he was being watched by those who would do him harm.

That's the way I feel today.

This is the sadness we have become.

Living by the Rule of Caesar

When I was in high school, I was required by Mrs. Lambert memorize bits and pieces of poetry and other famous literature. I hated it, probably because memorizing is not something I'm particularly good at. But I got a small benefit from it as watched the tributes to George H.W. Bush. One of the passages that we memorized was Marc Antony's funeral speech from Shakespeare's Julius Caesar.

The evil that men do lives after them; the good is oft interred with their bones.

It wasn't the tributes that reminded me of the passage so much as the reaction to them. Some people said that, since he had done a number of bad things in his presidency (and before), there should have been no such praise. The attacks brought to mind the end of the same speech.

O judgment! thou art fled to brutish beasts,
And men have lost their reason.

I was no fan of either George H.W. or George W.. I thought that they, especially George W. when he invaded Iraq, did a lot of harm to the country. But the things that I disagreed with didn't sum up their lives. I think both Bush's were honorable men who did what they thought right at the time. The fact that some of those things were proved not to be right by passing time is just proof of the value and validity of hind sight. But the fact that we judge people by a single aspect of their lives scares me.

I would like to think that I would be remembered better by people who know me than by my worst acts.

On the evening news, I saw where Chick-fil-a has been banned on the campus of some universities and in some cities because of the CEO's remarks about gay marriage. He's against it.

For most of my life I've tried to remember that, as a straight white guy, I had no right to tell minorities, LGBTQ people, or women what they should offended by. But this made me wonder. Here we had an institutional or governmental ban on a business because the CEO was on the wrong side of a controversial issue. (I say "the wrong side" because I, like most people these days, consider the side that I'm not on to be the wrong side. We've lost the capacity to say "the other side.")

However, he also runs a company that gives opportunities to young people, that provides a good product, and has been a good corporate citizen in Atlanta. When I was teaching Sunday School, one of my students worked at Chick-fil-a through high school, and they put him through college. After college, he went to work for them as a manager.

My question is: isn't there some sort of balance of actions and opinions? Do we ignore the good and act only on what we consider the bad?

This sort of tunnel vision is leading us into some strange areas.

President Trump, tweeting his opinion on the controversy regarding the Confederate memorials, said that next, they'll be coming for the memorials for Jefferson and Washington. My first thought was this made about as much sense as Trump usually makes, which is to say, not much. However, I've seen some people questioning the worth of Washington and Jefferson since they owned slaves.

Rationally, there's no equivalence between a memorial to Stonewall Jackson and a memorial to George Washington.

Jackson was a general in an army in rebellion against the United States. The Confederacy lost, and that made him a traitor. If the Confederacy had won, he would have been a patriot. We don't memorialize traitors.

Washington, on the other hand, led an army in rebellion against the British. We won. That made him a patriot. But…how about his slaves?

This is where we really run into a problem. We are judging him, a somewhat distant historical figure, by current standards. Most people today consider slavery to be illegal, inhuman, and beneath a civilized society. It wasn't that way in the 18th century in the South. Rich, white people owned slaves, and George Washington was a rich white person.

In the middle of the 19th century, shortly after the Southern Baptist Convention was founded, they were asked to rule on whether it was Christian to whip slaves. It was assumed that it was Christian to own slaves, but there was a question, at least in some minds, what the limits in dealing with them might be. The ruling was that since it was necessary to discipline slaves, one might whip a slave in a Christian manner.

Times have changed, and we might be thankful for that. But we shouldn't forget that times have changed.

I wish we could develop a more nuanced approach to judgment, if indeed we have to judge every act by every person we encounter. Most of our lives are some sort of assortment of good and bad, helpful and hurtful, useful and futile. And, if we feel compelled to act on our opinion of someone, I wish that we look at the balance of his or her life.

That doesn't mean we have to accept anything by anybody. There are people whom I choose not to talk to because I simply don't care for their opinions or the way they express them. That's the reason I've unfriended a few people on Facebook. But that's simply my exercising a personal prerogative. I don't suggest that they be banned, incarcerated, or otherwise punished. In fact, I have a great deal of respect for a couple of these people in other areas of their life.

We can choose our friends. Choose our television programs. Choose the forums in which we wish to participate. That's all personal.

But when we pick a single action, opinion, or attitude from somebody's life and damn them for it, I think we're setting a standard by which none of us can be judged as good.

Antony said that Caesar had been accused of being ambitious, but he had seen him weep with the poor, that he had been presented—and had refused—the crown on three occasions. Whether Caesar was ambitious or not, the good should not be interred with the bones while we remember only the evil.

What We Treasure Most

When I was a child—maybe six or seven years old—Dan Gilbert, Richard Britt and I used to play a game that involved which sense or body part we would choose to lose if we had to lose one. The arguments would be energetic: if you lost your sight you couldn't see to get around; if you lost your hearing, you wouldn't know what was around you in the dark; if you lost your legs you couldn't walk. We sit on the wall in front of Richard's house and argue for what seems like hours.

And now that I've grown old, I know that our answers were wrong.

We didn't even consider the most terrible thing to lose. It wasn't because we were dumb, but because we were young, too young to know their real value.

The most terrible thing to lose would be our memories, what has happened to get us to where we are.

I woke up early this morning and began paging through my memories. There are a lot of them, involving a small world of people, many of whom are no longer with us except as memories. That's the problem with getting very old, so many people who are important to us are no longer here.

But, as sad as that thought may be, the memories are not sad. Some of them recall actions more laudable than others, but they are the building blocks of a long life.